5 DAYS IN MAY

5 DAYS
IN MAY

THE COALITION
AND BEYOND

ANDREW ADONIS

Biteback Publishing

First published in Great Britain in 2013 by
Biteback Publishing Ltd
Westminster Tower
3 Albert Embankment
London SE1 7SP
Copyright © Andrew Adonis 2013

ISBN 978-1-84954-566-2

10 9 8 7 6 5 4 3 2 1

A CIP catalogue record for this book is available from the British Library.

Set in Adobe Garamond Pro

Printed and bound in Great Britain by
CPI Group (UK) Ltd, Croydon CR0 4YY

CONTENTS

7 DAYS IN MAY

5 DAYS IN MAY

INTRODUCTION

I wrote *5 Days in May* in the weeks immediately after the Cameron–Clegg coalition took office in 2010. As a post-election negotiator for Labour, I had a sense of their enduring historical importance and felt I should relate the tale as I had experienced it.

I did not publish the account at the time because in summer 2010 I was appointed Director of the Institute for Government, a cross-party think tank, and did not wish to return to post-election controversies. Now that I am back in the political fray I have no such inhibitions. Furthermore, the impending third anniversary of the coalition is a moment not only to take stock of the formation of the coalition but also to reflect on the experience of coalition since 2010 and its lessons for the future of the Labour Party in particular.

The book is divided into two parts. The first is the unaltered text of *5 Days in May*, which I wrote in June 2010. The second is my reflections on the Cameron–Clegg coalition, on the institution of coalition government more broadly and on the lessons for Labour. My conclusions are that, while coalitions can clearly be made to work in modern Britain, they are not preferable to single-party majority government either as a means of promoting national consensus and unity or as a means of providing strong government able to tackle big social and economic challenges.

This makes it all the more important for Labour to seek to win the next election on its own, as a broad One Nation coalition.

April 2013

DRAMATIS PERSONAE

Bob AINSWORTH – Defence Secretary in the Brown Cabinet 2010.

Danny ALEXANDER – Member of Lib Dem negotiating team in May 2010. Chief Secretary to the Treasury after David Laws's resignation on 29 May 2010.

Douglas ALEXANDER – International Development Secretary in the Brown Cabinet 2010.

Paddy ASHDOWN – Lib Dem leader 1988–99.

Ed BALLS – Principal Gordon Brown adviser 1994–2007. Children's Secretary 2007–10. Shadow Chancellor since 2011. Member of Labour negotiating team in May 2010.

Hilary BENN – Secretary of State for Environment, Food and Rural Affairs in Brown Cabinet 2010.

Tony BLAIR – Labour Prime Minister who won Commons majorities of 179 (1997), 167 (2001) and 66 (2005).

David BLUNKETT – Home Secretary and Education Secretary under Tony Blair.

Vernon BOGDANOR – Professor of Government at King's College London.

Adam BOULTON – Political editor, Sky News.

Ben BRADSHAW – Culture Secretary in Brown Cabinet 2010.

Leon BRITTAN – Cabinet Minister under Margaret Thatcher 1981–86. EU Commissioner 1989–99.

Gordon BROWN – Longest continuous resident of Downing Street since Lloyd George 1997–2010.

Iain BUNDRED – Special Adviser to Gordon Brown in No. 10.

Liam BYRNE – Chief Secretary to the Treasury in the Brown Cabinet 2010.

David CAMERON – Fourth Conservative leader in a row not to win a Commons majority. First peacetime coalition Prime Minister since the 1930s.

Alastair CAMPBELL – Communications Director to Tony Blair.

Ming CAMPBELL – Leader of the Lib Dems 2006–7.

Matt CAVANAGH – Special Adviser to Gordon Brown in No. 10.

Nick CLEGG – Leader of the Liberal Democrats since 2007. Most senior Liberal/Lib Dem minister since Lloyd George.

Greg COOK – Labour Party political strategist.

Yvette COOPER – Work and Pensions Secretary in the Brown Cabinet 2010.

Alistair DARLING – Chancellor of the Exchequer in the Brown Cabinet 2010.

John DENHAM – Secretary of State for Communities and Local Government in the Brown Cabinet 2010.

Justin FORSYTH – Communications and Campaigns Director for Gordon Brown in No. 10.

Sir Christopher GEIDT – Private Secretary to the Queen since 2007.

Philip GOULD – Labour strategist and pollster to Tony Blair and Gordon Brown.

Michael GOVE – Shadow Children's Secretary before May 2010; Secretary of State for Education since.

William HAGUE – Shadow Foreign Secretary before May 2010; Foreign Secretary since. Member of the Conservative negotiating team in May 2010.

Peter HAIN – Secretary of State for Wales in the Brown Cabinet 2010.

Harriet HARMAN – Deputy Leader of the Labour Party since 2007. Member of Labour's negotiating team in May 2010.

Robert HAZELL – Professor of Government and the Constitution at University College London since 1999.

Edward HEATH – Leader of the Conservative Party 1965–75. Prime Minister 1970–74. Leader of the only one-term government since 1931.

Sir Jeremy HEYWOOD – Permanent Secretary, No. 10, under Brown and Cameron. Cabinet Secretary since 2012.

Simon HUGHES – Lib Dem MP. Deputy Leader of the Lib Dems since 2010.

Chris HUHNE – Energy and Climate Change Secretary, 2010–12. Member of Lib Dem negotiating team in May 2010.

Derry IRVINE (Lord Irvine of Lairg) – Pupil master and mentor of Tony Blair. Lord Chancellor 1997–2003.

Joe IRVINE – Special Adviser to Gordon Brown in
No. 10.

Roy JENKINS – Labour Home Secretary and Chancellor
under Wilson and Callaghan. President of the European
Commission 1977–81. Leader of the SDP, 1982–3.

Alan JOHNSON – Home Secretary in the Brown Cabinet
2010. Shadow Chancellor 2010–11.

Tessa JOWELL – Minister for the Olympics in the Brown
Cabinet 2010.

Gavin KELLY – Deputy Chief of Staff to Gordon Brown
in No. 10.

Charles KENNEDY – Leader of the Lib Dems 1999–2006.

Sadiq KHAN – Minister for Transport in the Brown
government 2010. Shadow Secretary of State for Justice
since 2010.

Sir Mervyn KING – Governor of the Bank of England
2003–13.

Jim KNIGHT (Lord Knight of Weymouth) – Minister for
Employment in the Brown government 2010.

Laura KUENSSBERG – Chief political correspondent for
BBC News in 2010.

David LAWS – Member of Lib Dem negotiating team
in May 2010, then briefly Chief Secretary to the Treasury.
Author of *22 Days in May*.

Oliver LETWIN – Minister for Policy since 2010. Member
of Tory negotiating team in May 2010.

Tony LLOYD – Chair of the Parliamentary Labour Party
2006–12.

Caroline LUCAS – Green Party MP for Brighton Pavilion since 2010.

Siobhain MCDONAGH – Labour MP.

Kirsty MCNEILL – Special Adviser to Gordon Brown in No. 10.

Peter MANDELSON (Lord Mandelson of Foy) – Secretary of State for Business, Innovation and Skills in the Brown Cabinet 2010. Member of Labour negotiating team in May 2010. Author of *The Third Man: Life at the Heart of New Labour* (2010).

John MANN – Labour MP.

Andrew MARR – Journalist and political commentator for the BBC in 2010.

David MILIBAND – Foreign Secretary 2007–10. Labour leadership runner-up, September 2010.

Ed MILIBAND – Energy and Climate Change Secretary in the Brown Cabinet 2010. Member of Labour negotiating team in May 2010. Leader of the Labour Party since September 2010.

David MUIR – Special Adviser to Gordon Brown in No. 10.

Rupert MURDOCH – Chairman and CEO of News Corporation.

Jim MURPHY – Secretary of State for Scotland in the Brown Cabinet 2010. Shadow Defence Secretary since 2010.

Sue NYE – Personal Assistant and Special Adviser to Gordon Brown in No. 10.

Jonny OATES – Director of General Election Communications for the Lib Dems 2010.

Sir Gus O'DONNELL – Cabinet Secretary 2005–11.

George OSBORNE – Shadow Chancellor before May 2010. Member of the Tory negotiating team in May 2010. Chancellor since 2010.

Jeremy PAXMAN – Presenter of *University Challenge* and *Newsnight*.

Nick PEARCE – Head of No. 10 Policy Unit under Gordon Brown.

John REID – Home Secretary under Tony Blair.

Sir David RICHARDS – Head of the British Army 2008–10. Chief of the Defence Staff since October 2010.

Sir Peter RICKETTS – Permanent Secretary of the Foreign and Commonwealth Office 2006–10. National Security Adviser to the Prime Minister 2010–12.

Nick ROBINSON – Political editor of the BBC since 2005.

Peter ROBINSON – Leader of the Democratic Unionist Party and First Minister of Northern Ireland since 2008.

Jan ROYALL (Baroness Royall of Blaisdon) – Leader of the House of Lords in the Brown Cabinet 2010. Shadow Leader of the House of Lords since 2010.

Alex SALMOND – Leader of the Scottish National Party. First Minister of Scotland since 2007.

Neil SHERLOCK – Adviser to successive Lib Dem leaders.

Robert SKIDELSKY (Lord Skidelsky) – Crossbench life peer, economic historian and author.

Andy SLAUGHTER – Labour MP.

Tim SNOWBALL – Lib Dem official. Managed Nick Clegg's election tour 2010.

Jon SOPEL – Political correspondent for the BBC.

David STEEL (Lord Steel of Aikwood) – Leader of the Liberal Party 1976–88.

Jack STRAW – Justice Secretary in the Brown Cabinet 2010.

Gisela STUART – Labour MP.

Andrew STUNELL – Member of Lib Dem negotiating team in 2010. Lib Dem junior minister 2010–12.

Margaret THATCHER – The last Conservative leader to win a majority of more than 21 (1979, 1983 and 1987).

Gareth THOMAS – Minister for International Development in the Brown government 2010.

Jeremy THORPE – Leader of the Liberal Party 1967–76.

David TRIESMAN (Lord Triesman) – General Secretary of the Labour Party 2001–3. Junior minister under Blair and Brown.

Shriti VADERA – Adviser to Gordon Brown.

Kirsty WARK – BBC journalist; presenter of *Newsnight*.

Stewart WOOD (Lord Wood of Anfield) – Special Adviser to Gordon Brown in No. 10. Adviser to Ed Miliband since 2010.

Tony WOODLEY – General Secretary of Unite 2007–11.

Shaun WOODWARD – Northern Ireland Secretary in the Brown Cabinet 2010.

Tony WRIGHT – Labour MP until 2010.

PREFACE

The inconclusive result of the general election held on 6 May 2010 precipitated one of the great dramas of modern British politics. It lasted five days, while Gordon Brown and David Cameron vied for Nick Clegg's support to form a government. This book tells the tale from the vantage point of 10 Downing Street, where I spent the five days at Gordon Brown's side.

Great dramas are about fateful choices and their consequences. This drama turned on two fateful choices: David Cameron's choice to forge a coalition with Nick Clegg rather than seek to form a minority Tory government; and Clegg's choice to align the Liberal Democrats with the Conservatives rather than with Labour.

A sheen of inevitability attaches to historic decisions after the event. It is rarely authentic, and certainly not in this case. In these five days choices were made rapidly, even instinctively, in the heat of extreme pressure, but they were made. The consequences will be played out over years, perhaps decades, to come.

30 June 2010

POLLING DAY, THURSDAY 6 MAY

'**W**e've got to stop Cameron and the media simply calling it for the Tories as soon as the exit poll is out tonight. How do we get it out there that even if they are the largest party, but there's no majority, they can't just walk into Downing Street and demand the keys? We've got to get onto the BBC now, so they're in the right place. Otherwise we'll be out of the game before it's even started.'

It was 9 a.m. and the third call of polling day morning from Gordon Brown, pacing around his Scottish constituency home in North Queensferry, working out how to get talks going with Nick Clegg if the election result was a hung parliament.

The possibility of Lab–Lib partnership had been a preoccupation of Gordon's since becoming Prime Minister in 2007. After the economic and political meltdown of 2008/9, it looked pretty fanciful that the Conservatives would not win an outright majority. The banking crisis, the recession, the scandal of MPs' expenses, and Gordon's personal unpopularity constantly reinforced each other. But in early 2010 the recession and the expenses crisis receded, and the polls narrowed in the run-up to the general election and during the campaign itself.

I said there needed to be commentators on the news alongside the exit poll, explaining the constitutional position that the sitting Prime Minister stays in No. 10 until there is a replacement government likely to command a Commons majority.

'That's it. Vernon Bogdanor and Robert Hazell. They're the experts. You should get onto them. I will speak to them…'

'No, Gordon, that's not a good idea,' I cut in. 'You need to be one stage removed from all this. I'll speak to them, and Justin [Forsyth] also needs to take Nick Robinson [the BBC's political editor] through it.'

'OK, but we've got to get this moving. They'll stop at nothing to get us out. The BBC will want big stuff to report in Downing Street in the morning whatever the result.'

•••

'Look, Andrew, it's simply not going to happen,' said Peter Mandelson. 'The Tories are going to win. That's been the position for months – two years – now, and it's still what's going to happen one way or another. And I tell you, if the country wakes up on Saturday morning and Labour is still there, there will be a wave of national revulsion.'

It was now noon on polling day, in a side office in Labour's deserted election headquarters in Victoria Street. I simply couldn't get Peter to take a hung parliament seriously, as I couldn't the week before, when I got a similar reaction. So

I had another go. 'We've got a duty to do this, Peter; there has got to be a government tomorrow and we may have to be part of it – we can't simply give up.'

'As for your Lib Dems, let me tell you about Paddy [Ashdown],' Peter sighed. 'Paddy was on the same train as Gordon and me, returning from the Newcastle rally last Saturday. So I went and plonked myself down next to him. He couldn't get away from me fast enough. It was as if I was a leper. He suddenly needed to go to the lavatory; to speak on his mobile; to do anything but speak to me or be seen with me. That's what your Lib Dems think about talking to Gordon.'

'I know all about that,' I countered. The story I heard was that Paddy had been in First Class while GB and entourage were in Standard Class, as throughout the election campaign. Much hilarity about the Lib Dems living the high life.

'I've had a similar brush-off from Paddy and the lot of them,' I said. 'That's their position until the polls close. It's a completely different position tomorrow if no one has a majority, as looks to me very likely. Let me tell you my thinking about how we handle it if that happens. Please just humour me and take it seriously.'

'OK', said Peter, opening his foolscap notebook, donning his reading glasses and taking notes as I spoke, his telltale signs of engagement. He was taking charge.

•••

I had phoned Paddy at 8.30 a.m. that morning. 'So it's Andrew Adonis; I wondered when you would ring,' was his greeting, speaking over the background clatter of the Yeovil Lib Dem campaign HQ, where he was campaigning for David Laws, his successor as the constituency's MP.

'Should we be meeting today for a private chat about life after tomorrow?' I ventured.

'Yes, we should.'

He was coming up to London to do the election-night programmes, so we arranged to meet at his house in Kennington at 5 p.m. At least, that was the plan until he called back ten minutes later.

'I have just spoken to my leader. I have got to be a team player…' – 'So am I, of course, that's why I contacted you,' I interjected – 'indeed, we are both team players,' Paddy continued, 'but my team doesn't want any contact whatever while the election is on, so it can't be today. How about 10 a.m. tomorrow, matchsticks all round?'

'Done, see you then.'

Two steps forward, one back.

So too with Danny Alexander, Nick Clegg's Chief of Staff. I barely knew Danny and had to get his mobile number on polling day morning from Neil Sherlock, an Oxford university friend who went into the City and was a trusted adviser to successive Lib Dem leaders, playing David Cameron in Nick Clegg's rehearsals for the TV election debates. Neil and I had talked at length about post-election possibilities. Like most senior Lib Dems, he was an instinctive Lib–Labber and anti-Tory.

'The problem is that I simply don't see how we can do a deal with Gordon Brown, who will have been rejected by the voters and is intensely disliked by Nick,' was Neil's view. 'But if that issue could be dealt with somehow…'

When Neil gave me Danny's number, he also asked me for Peter Mandelson's to pass on to Danny. I texted Danny at the same time as phoning Paddy. No response – until 8.30 p.m. when Danny replied: 'Would be good to talk privately later this evening.'

•••

By then, Gordon Brown was catching a few hours' sleep in North Queensferry, which was to make him the only non-exhausted member of his team by the end of the long night to come.

The Tories were briefing hard that with voter turn-out sharply up they were on course for a small majority. Shortly after 9 p.m. came leaks of an exit poll putting the Conservatives on 39 per cent – 'which will clinch it for them', Peter Mandelson said.

Gordon had been on the phone for most of the preceding hours, laying the ground for possible Lab–Libbery to come. Key trade union leaders and Cabinet ministers were squared for the principle of negotiations if the Tories were well short of a majority. None dissented in principle. Justin had no difficulty with Nick Robinson. The BBC were clear that they would not call the election for Cameron until the Tories had won an overall majority or close to one; and they would stand by GB's right and duty to remain in No. 10 until a new government was formed.

'Good. That makes it harder for Cameron to do a Salmond,' remarked Gordon when we spoke in the early evening.

'Doing a Salmond' was shorthand for the immediate peril he foresaw if the Tories were the largest party but even some way short of a majority. Alex Salmond propelled himself into the leadership of a minority Scottish government after the 2007 Scottish Parliament election, immediately proclaiming it 'the worst defeat for Labour in fifty years and a victory for the SNP' and demanding the SNP's right to power. In fact, the SNP ended up only one seat ahead of Labour and well short of a majority. But the media endlessly recycled 'the worst Labour result for fifty years', and paved the way for Salmond to become First Minister.

Gordon also did conference calls with Gavin Kelly and Nick Pearce, his policy directors, on negotiating positions for talks with the Lib Dems.

'There isn't a policy problem here,' he said, phoning me afterwards, as we discussed different options for a referendum on electoral reform and tax changes, which the Lib Dems would want. 'There will be other problems' – we both knew he was talking about his own position; neither mentioned it at this stage – 'but the key thing is to get them talking to us at the same time as the Tories, not afterwards. And to get going in the morning. Every delay helps the Tories. How are we doing on that?'

'There's still the Clegg doctrine,' I said uneasily. 'But at least we have got contacts in place to get going immediately.'

'OK, let's speak as soon as the results start.'

The 'Clegg doctrine' was shorthand for Nick Clegg's

election statement that in a hung parliament the first chance to form a government should go to the largest party in terms of seats and votes. There is no such constitutional convention; nor does this necessarily happen in Continental countries with coalitions. Willy Brandt's great government was a coalition between the second-placed SPD and the liberal FDP; the current Swedish Conservative government is led by the second largest party, a long way behind the Social Democrats in seats and votes. So we assumed that Clegg had mis-spoken or deliberately strengthened his anti-Labour position for the TV election debates, where he resisted every invitation to 'agree with Gordon' even where he plainly did so.

Either way, we thought, surely if given the choice, Clegg wouldn't put the Tories in power, throwing over a British Liberal tradition going back a century and a half as a progressive anti-Tory party?

FRIDAY 7 MAY

Gordon Brown was still asleep when, just after 10 p.m., the BBC broadcast its exit poll projecting a hung parliament with the Tories nineteen seats short of an overall majority.

This was better for Labour than anticipated by most of the party's own campaign team, let alone the media. Cheering erupted in the party's Victoria Street headquarters. David Muir, one of Gordon's key strategists, hugged the party's veteran pollster Philip Gould, 'it is so good'.

Everyone thought the exit poll underestimated the Lib Dems. Surely they weren't going down from sixty-four to fifty-nine seats after three weeks of Cleggmania following the first TV debate between the party leaders? But if the Lib Dems were doing better than fifty-nine, then the 307 projected for the Tories might be an over-estimate, pulling them even further from the magic 326 needed for an overall majority and giving Labour, projected at 255 seats, a chance of a majority with the Lib Dems.

So it was in a mood of optimistic uncertainty that, shortly before 11 p.m., Gordon's aides who had finished the campaign with him in Scotland at a boisterous rally in Kirkcaldy on Wednesday night – including Sue Nye, his longest-serving aide; Justin Forsyth and Iain Bundred, his media staff; Kirsty McNeill, his speechwriter; and Stewart Wood, a policy adviser – headed from the King Malcolm Hotel to his detached red-brick constituency home on the hilltop overlooking North Queensferry and the Firth of Forth.

When they arrived the only person downstairs was Sarah Brown, watching a film. 'I suppose we had better get moving,' she remarked laconically as she went upstairs to wake Gordon. The team set up in the dining room to make calls while awaiting the first constituency results. These were late coming through because of the increased turnout which led to long queues and voters being turned away when polling stations closed at 10 p.m.

The first results after 11 p.m., from Sunderland in Labour's north-eastern heartland, painted a confused picture. The swings against Labour were 8.4 per cent and 11.5 per cent in the first two – very safe Labour – seats to be declared, but less than 5 per cent in Sunderland Central, the constituency competitive with the Tories, which Labour held. A swing to the Tories of less than 5 per cent in marginal seats was hung parliament territory. This picture of differential swings, with sitting Labour MPs in tight fights with the Tories often keeping the swing down and holding their seats, soon became a recurring pattern. So after an initial flurry that it was all over, the mood shifted to watching and waiting in the hope that the exit poll was right after all.

As expected, the Tories tried at the outset to 'do a Salmond'. George Osborne, Michael Gove and other Tory talking heads kept repeating the mantra that Labour was heading for its 'worst result since 1931' and had been overwhelmingly rejected. But the Salmond strategy fizzled around 1 a.m. as Labour holds were declared or predicted in weathervane seats like Gedling in Nottinghamshire, Telford in Shropshire, Bolton North-East in Greater Manchester and Tooting in South London, with remarkably strong Labour performances across Scotland and North Wales. The BBC held to its projection of a hung parliament with the Tories a good way short of a majority and the likelihood of inter-party negotiations to follow.

•••

The prime ministerial convoy left Ferryhills Road at midnight for the half-hour journey to Gordon Brown's constituency count at Kirkcaldy's Adam Smith College. Gordon was working in the back of the car on the critical passage of his acceptance speech on the national picture.

'It's all up in the air,' he said, calling from the car.

We discussed emerging hung parliament scenarios. If the Tories did no better than the exit poll's 307, we should explore a coalition with the Lib Dems.

'The key thing', I said, 'is to be clear that you have no option here. It's your duty now to ensure orderly talks between the parties, leading if possible to a sustainable government commanding a majority.'

We rehearsed different lines and settled on the imperative for 'strong, stable and principled government' – 'strong and stable' meaning a coalition, not a minority Tory government, and 'principled' implying an agreement between like-minded parties, i.e. Labour and the Lib Dems. These were the key words in Gordon's constituency declaration speech at 1.30 a.m., which ran throughout the overnight election coverage thereafter.

The next move in the chess game was David Cameron's speech at his Witney constituency declaration at 3 a.m. He struck an uncertain note, deliberately so, I thought. Although Labour had 'lost its mandate to govern' and the Tories were 'on target to win more seats than in the last eighty years', he did not call for Gordon Brown's immediate resignation and he suggested that it could be a while before a new government emerged. 'What will guide me in the hours ahead – and perhaps longer than hours ahead – is to do what is right for our country … At all times I will put the national interest first to make sure we have good, strong, stable government for our country.'

'It's certainly not an immediate Salmond strategy,' I said to GB when we next spoke. 'I wonder whether he's also thinking of a play for the Lib Dems.'

•••

Surrounding GB's constituency declaration was a 'purple patch' of good Labour results which lasted for another hour or so. By now Scotland, amazingly, was showing an overall swing to Labour.

It was thus a fairly buoyant Team Brown which headed from his count to the Labour celebration at a local community centre. So much so that as he arrived, a mobile phone call to Peter Robinson – the Northern Ireland DUP leader, who lost his East Belfast seat on a massive hostile swing in the wake of his wife Iris's affairs – had to be aborted because of whooping and cheering at the defeat of Willie Rennie, the Lib Dem who had won a by-election in the neighbouring seat to Gordon's in Dunfermline & West Fife. Gordon retreated to a cupboard behind the reception to convey his personal regrets to Robinson, and reassurances of his continued confidence in his leadership of the Northern Ireland Assembly.

Shortly before 3 a.m. the prime ministerial convoy left for Edinburgh Airport and the flight to London. Planning for the morning started in earnest.

'I need you all in No. 10 in the morning,' Gordon said to Stewart Wood. 'It's business as usual, and we need to get talks going with the Liberals as soon as possible.' (He always referred to 'the Liberals' never 'the Lib Dems', which annoyed Nick Clegg and other Lib Dems.)

The 'immediate resignation' statement – one of three which Kirsty McNeill had drafted on her laptop – was left untouched. Work started instead on a statement opening negotiations with the Lib Dems. (This was another Gordon Brown characteristic: always to be working on the text of his next speech or statement. It did not cease until moments before his final resignation speech five days later.)

•••

Bad results were coming in with the good. Just before mobiles had to be switched off on the plane for take-off at 3.30 a.m., there were reports of several narrow defeats. 'That's bad organisation on the ground, that is,' GB snapped in irritation. But he remained confident and gave an upbeat briefing to journalists at the back of the plane. 'I have been through a lot in my political career and my personal life,' he told them. 'I am used to difficulty. Difficulty is not an excuse for failure. But difficulty does not set you back. It is what prompts you to move forward with more determination … What is clear is that the expectations of the Conservative Party have not been met.'

When mobiles were switched on again as the plane taxied to a stand at Stansted an hour later, the bad news was uppermost. A Tory swathe was being cut through the East and West Midlands and southern England. A succession of Lib Dems – in their more rural and slower to count constituencies – were also falling to the Tories, starting to bear out the exit poll in that decisive respect.

It looked to be slipping away after all. On landing, Justin Forsyth immediately tweeted: 'Just landed back in London. Lots of results coming in. But picture still not clear. Gordon focused on stable, strong and principled gov.' But GB himself looked crestfallen – 'the only time I remember him like this in the whole election', said one aide. 'He wasn't angry as at Rochdale [after his inadvertently recorded 'bigot' remarks about Mrs Duffy], but he clearly thought the game was up, and so did we.'

'Our problem is that the Liberals are just too weak against

the Tories,' Gordon said to me on the phone as his convoy left Stansted. 'I always knew this would be our big problem – not all that *Guardian* stuff about Clegg coming second – which is why I wanted to do that deal with them,' he added. He was referring to his pre-election idea of standing Labour candidates down in thirty Lib Dem–Conservative marginals, a suggestion rebuffed strongly by his campaign team in the days immediately before the election.

The mood wasn't lightened by the convoy getting lost on the journey into London, taking the wrong exit off the A13 at Royal Docks and having to go the whole way round a roundabout to double back, under the whirring gaze of the ever-present media helicopter.

However, as London approached and the sun rose, the news brightened. London results were starting to come through, and these were surprisingly good. Andy Slaughter held on with a relatively small swing against Labour in Hammersmith, as did Gareth Thomas in Harrow. Gisela Stuart's spectacular hold in Birmingham Edgbaston was a further tonic. Cabinet ministers Ed Balls, John Denham and Ben Bradshaw all survived in seats that could easily have gone Tory. By the time Gordon arrived in Victoria Street at 5.30 a.m., to be clapped in by Peter Mandelson, Alastair Campbell, Harriet Harman and the party staff, it was possibly game on again.

After a short speech of thanks to party workers, GB decamped to a side office with Peter, Alastair and the party's pollster, Greg Cook. The room was strewn with half-eaten takeaway meals and overnight debris.

'The key thing is that we and the Liberals have got more

seats than the Tories,' said Gordon. 'Is that going to continue to be the case?' he asked Greg.

'It looks like it,' said Greg. 'It's looking like 313 at least for Labour plus the Lib Dems, with the Tories on low 300s.'

'In that case, we need to get going with Clegg; we'll be fine with the minor parties,' said Gordon.

Peter was downbeat and dejected. But as Gordon went through the numbers – 'we can absolutely do this, Peter' – he came round to the possibility. 'But Nick Clegg will be very bruised by this result, you are going to have to treat him very carefully,' Peter cautioned.

It was agreed that Peter would head to the studios to do a round of interviews keeping Gordon and Labour in play. Gordon would go back to No. 10, making no further statement, to catch some sleep while his aides re-established his office for the morning to come.

•••

While Gordon was driven back to No. 10, filmed entering through the front door, key members of his staff entered through the 70 Whitehall entrance to the Cabinet Office, which leads to a back entrance to No. 10. Gavin Kelly, Nick Pearce, David Muir and Joe Irvine 'had practically to break into No. 10', one of them recalled. The government car bringing in Jeremy Heywood, the ubiquitous, brilliant linchpin of Downing Street's official machine, was late. A doorkeeper, a duty clerk and a messenger constituted the nerve centre of government at 7 a.m.

When the four aides entered the large open-plan 'war room' in No. 10, they found that their desks had been moved. When they tried to log onto the No. 10 computer system, their user accounts had been deleted. They officially existed no more. 'The King is dead; long live the King', one of them muttered.

But perhaps the King was not yet dead after all. They plugged in their portable laptops and printers and got to work.

•••

'Is a deal still possible?' Nick Robinson texted me at 3.26 a.m. 'I assume phones are already buzzing between parties.'

'Everything looks possible', I texted back.

But as yet there was no buzzing of phones between Labour and the Lib Dems, at least. While GB and entourage were closeted in Victoria Street discussing the realm of the possible, I was heading to White City for ninety minutes with Jeremy Paxman, saying as little as possible beyond the need for 'a strong, stable and principled government'.

Escaping at 6.20 a.m., I phoned Danny Alexander, not having replied to his text the previous evening. He was going through security at Inverness Airport ('I've got to surrender this phone imminently, even if you're still Transport Secretary'), on his way from his constituency to London, and called back ten minutes later.

I said Gordon was ready to start talks whenever Nick Clegg was ready, and we hoped it could be in parallel with any Tory discussions. Danny was reassuring. 'We are licking our wounds and Nick isn't planning to say anything much apart from thanking party workers at Cowley Street [the Lib Dems' London headquarters] until all the results are in at lunchtime.' I said that GB wasn't planning to say anything substantive either until there had been further contact later in the morning.

The position nonetheless looked precarious. Paddy called at 9.10 a.m. to cancel our meeting scheduled for 10 a.m.

'I need to be with my guys,' he said with typical brusqueness. 'The problem is the numbers don't seem to be there for the two of us to do business.'

I didn't demur, except to say that it was too soon to be sure and we needed to take stock when we got the final numbers.

'OK, let's think about it further and speak later.'

A similar call followed from David Laws, still in Yeovil. David and I had first met when helping, for our respective parties, to negotiate the Lab–Lib coalition which took office after the first Scottish Parliament elections in 1999. Since then, through a long spell when he was my shadow at Education, we had become friends.

'It all looks pretty difficult,' David said.

I pushed back harder than with Paddy. 'But won't it be harder for you to prop up the Tories?'

'I'm not sure that's right,' he responded immediately, having clearly considered this. 'If we go in with you, in a precarious numbers game, and it all collapses in a mess, then we may be worse off than letting the Tories come in and trying to control them.'

'But David, they're the Tories, and how are you going to control them?'

'I know, I know. But it may be the best course open to us.'

Again we agreed to stay in touch and I set off for the war room in No. 10.

•••

Although fully part of the No. 10 rabbit warren of state rooms, private apartments and working offices, Gordon Brown's large war room – as everyone called it – was geographically in No. 12 Downing Street, the next 'house' along the street from the Chancellor's at No. 11. No. 12 has a front door onto Downing Street, but this is unused and it is reached by a connecting corridor from the front hallway of No. 10, passing through the narrow hallway of No. 11. The doors between the three houses were kept open.

The light wood-panelled conference room in No. 12 is by far the largest of the working offices in Downing Street, occupying almost the entire ground floor of the building as viewed from the rear gates of Downing Street opening onto Horse Guards Road and St James's Park. For decades it had been the sparsely used office of the government whips until Alastair Campbell annexed it for his expanding No. 10 media operation during Tony Blair's second term. Alastair took for himself the elegant wood-panelled corner office overlooking St James's Park on one side and the walled Downing Street garden on the other, which had been the

Chief Whip's office, while his cohorts were massed in the conference room next door.

Gordon got the idea of 'going open-plan' from Mayor Michael Bloomberg of New York, who ran both his media empire and New York this way and swore by its positive impact on team building, information sharing and the rapid taking and implementation of decisions. Gordon moved out of the study next to the Cabinet Room, the 'den' which Tony Blair had used as his office for most of his three terms, with its famous sofas, and relocated to the No. 12 open-plan together with his private secretaries, duty clerks and key political and media advisers, most of whom had previously been spread out in poky offices on various floors of No. 10.

Gordon's own desk was in the centre of a horseshoe of desks facing out from the long side of the war room, close to the doorway leading into Alastair's old office, which Gordon used for more private meetings and phone calls. However, he was usually to be found in the open-plan, Jeremy Heywood at the desk to his left and Justin Forsyth to the right. When not in conversation with staff or on the phone, he would be sending or reading emails, or tapping away at draft speeches or statements in large block capitals visible to those passing behind. For those sitting at the desks in front, a large forehead protruding from a PC was the view of the Prime Minister. Behind him, above, was a giant TV screen with Sky News on constant feed, facing a screen on the opposite wall set to BBC News 24. One aide likened the scene to the bridge of the Starship *Enterprise*.

The 'war room' was teeming when I arrived at 10 a.m.

Gordon had just come down from his flat after a two-hour nap, hair dishevelled, shirt open, but the liveliest politician in the room. (He became more so as the rest of us flagged.) Peter Mandelson was back from his media round. Alastair Campbell was standing by Gordon's desk ('Well, home from home – and all at the beck and call of your pesky Liberals,' his cheery greeting). Jeremy Heywood was in hushed phone conversation at his desk, as for much of the next five days, often with the Queen's Private Secretary at the Palace or with Sir Gus O'Donnell, the Cabinet Secretary, who was located in the Cabinet Office but ventured periodically through the maze of interconnecting corridors and security-controlled doors to visit the war room.

We debated Clegg's and Cameron's likely first moves.

Gordon was insistent: 'We've got to get this going with the Liberals – there's got to be movement today and something settled over the weekend or Cameron will simply take possession.'

His first public step, taken shortly after 10 a.m., was an official government statement that he had instructed the Cabinet Secretary 'to arrange for civil servants to provide support for parties engaged in discussion'. This followed the Cabinet Office guidelines on procedure in a hung parliament, which Gus O'Donnell had framed in February in collaboration with Christopher Geidt, the Queen's Private Secretary, and constitutional experts.

Widely publicised at the time, these guidelines were intended to condition expectations against a sitting Prime Minister resigning after the election unless and until it was clear, through negotiations with other parties as necessary, that he could not command a Commons majority but the Leader of the Opposition could do so. By explicitly stating that the sitting Prime Minister should remain in office while inter-party talks took place and until a conclusion was reached which could be recommended by him to the Queen, the aim was to keep the Palace clear of controversy and create the space for orderly negotiations. The guidelines served this purpose pretty well in the five days ahead.

This initial statement was briefed and reported as signifying that Gordon would not be resigning imminently, although no longer leader of the largest party. There was no immediate push back from the Tories. Indeed there was no word from the Conservatives at all. David Cameron, we presumed, was holed up debating next steps, much as we were.

•••

This statement out, Gordon started calculating 'the numbers' on a jotter pad in his thick black felt-tip pen. 'The numbers' – the tally of MPs supporting different possible combinations in the House of Commons – were to be a constant refrain of the next five days.

By Friday lunchtime the final tally of seats by party was to be: Conservative 306 (plus one likely Tory seat to be filled at a separate election), Labour 258, Lib Dem 57 and others 28 – almost identical to the exit poll those fifteen long hours before.

So there wasn't an overall Lab–Lib majority to be had. The Lab–Lib total was 315; an overall majority 326. On Friday morning almost everyone's first reaction to this emerging picture – including those of us in the war room – was that therefore only a 'rainbow alliance' of virtually everyone besides the Tories could keep David Cameron out. And that the grubby deals necessary with the Scots and Welsh Nationalists, and the various Ulster parties, put this idea beyond the pale.

But by 10.30, GB had deconstructed the projected numbers to produce a different and radically more positive picture.

Gordon's premise was that virtually all the minor-party MPs would either support Labour or abstain on confidence and other critical votes, without the need for deals, grubby or otherwise.

For the vital initial vote on the Queen's Speech, a Lab–Lib government would command (on the basis of the final tally of numbers) between 330 and 338 votes, with only the Tories' 307 against, giving a comfortable majority of between twenty-three and thirty-one. Also, for working purposes the majority threshold was not 326 but 322 or 323, once the Speaker, his deputies and the five absent Sinn Fein MPs were factored in. So the Lab–Lib 315 would not only outvote the Tories' 307, but was enough to control ordinary business, on realistic assumptions about the behaviour of the smaller parties, including the steady support likely to be forthcoming from the five SDLP, Alliance and Independent members from Northern Ireland, who were either soulmates of the Left or instinctively hostile to the Tories.

As Gordon set out his view of 'the numbers', it sounded plausible.

The nine Scottish and Welsh Nationalist MPs, he put it bluntly, 'would not dare vote against us; they'd be killed in Scotland and Wales in next year's elections [for the Scottish Parliament and the Welsh Assembly] if they put the Tories in'. As he would often put it over the coming days, 'The SNP still haven't recovered from putting in Thatcher in 1979 and this election was fought in Scotland as if Thatcher was about to come to power again.' Both the SNP and Plaid Cymru made statements later on Friday supporting this view. The new Green MP, Caroline Lucas, was also naturally anti-Tory. Then there were the five naturally pro-Labour Ulster MPs.

As for Ulster's nine DUP members, they were at daggers drawn with the Tories over David Cameron's decision to forge an alliance between the Tories and the Ulster Unionist Party to fight the DUP. The 2010 election was the first time the Conservatives had mobilised in Ulster since the Official Unionist Party severed its link with the Tories back in the Heath era in the 1970s. By contrast, GB had built good relations with Peter Robinson and the DUP over years of patient peace-process diplomacy. Shaun Woodward, the Northern Ireland Secretary, said that Robinson would be supportive without any formal deal, 'subject to the usual arguments about money, but we have those in any event'.

We wrote down the new numbers. 'This gives us a serious play,' Peter agreed. 'The numbers' became the opening gambit in countless conversations to come about Lab–Libbery.

None of us thought it would be easy. Alex Salmond's six SNP MPs would be relentlessly opportunist. As for the Lab–Lib core of 315, this was fine if our MPs were united and hungry for power, but thirteen years on from 'glad confident morning', serial malcontents were a constant problem. 'We've had knife-edge votes every few weeks with a paper majority of fifty, so how do we keep this show on the road?' said one aide, weary from years of backbench arm-twisting.

There was also the 'Gordon issue', as it was euphemistically termed in the inner circle. On the Friday, no one knew how this was to be resolved. But everyone knew that an arrangement with the Lib Dems was impossible unless it was.

However, all depended on whether the Lib Dems wanted to engage with us in the first place. If they did, a stark choice could immediately be presented to Labour MPs: do we seek to govern with willing Lib Dem partners, or do we hand the country over to the Tories gratuitously? 'It's a strange idea that the way to gain power is to give it away; the Tories never make that mistake,' was my line. When formal discussions with the Lib Dems finally started on Day Four (Monday evening), and both the Cabinet and the party's National Executive Committee debated this fundamental issue, there was little dissent to the principle of engagement.

But from the Lib Dems on that Friday morning of Day One came ominous silence.

Danny Alexander hadn't got back to Peter or to me with any suggested first step, and he wasn't returning calls. As we discussed options, a news alert flashed across Sky News.

Nick Clegg would make a statement when he arrived at the
Lib Dems' Cowley Street HQ from his Sheffield constituency at about 10.30 a.m.

I relayed my 7 a.m. conversation with Danny: he didn't
think Clegg would say anything much until all the results
were in. 'Why big it up as a statement then?' said Gordon.
Why indeed? Anticipation mounted as a media helicopter
tracked the Lib Dem leader's car from St Pancras station to
Westminster.

•••

Nick Clegg's statement, delivered noteless and tired, was a
decisive opening towards the Conservatives. He restated in
terms his election campaign statement that 'whichever party
gets the most votes and the most seats, if not an absolute
majority, has the first right to seek to govern', and went on:
'I think it is now for the Conservative Party to prove that it
is capable of seeking to govern in the national interest.'

Barely had Clegg finished than another news alert flashed
across the screen: David Cameron would make a statement
at 2.30 p.m.

Our immediate assumption was that these statements
were not co-ordinated. We expected Cameron at 2.30,
with the results complete, to call on GB to make way for
a Conservative government. He would then reach whatever accommodation he could with the Lib Dems and the
other parties.

'I've got to make a statement before Cameron,' said

Gordon, watching the unfolding news on Sky. 'We've got to forestall him simply claiming power, and set out an expectation that there will now be talks between the parties. And we've got to get a process started with Clegg today.'

We rapidly decided on GB making a statement at 1.30 p.m. GB's concern was to demonstrate that he was still governing, dealing with the crisis over Greece and the euro ('I need to speak to Alistair [Darling], and then to Sarkozy, Trichet [President of the European Central Bank], and Strauss-Kahn [managing director of the International Monetary Fund]', he instructed a Private Secretary), and to say that he intended to speak to Clegg.

Gordon also needed to rise above the fray in his constitutional duty to pave the way for a new government. He had therefore to respect the right of Clegg to speak first to Cameron. We decided to state this in terms ('I understand and completely respect the position of Mr Clegg in stating that he wishes first to make contact with the leader of the Conservative Party'), and to make a virtue of this as the first stage in a process ('Mr Cameron and Mr Clegg should clearly be entitled to take as much time as they feel necessary') which we hoped would lead rapidly on to Lab–Lib talks ('clearly, should the discussions between Mr Cameron and Mr Clegg come to nothing, then I would of course be prepared to discuss with Mr Clegg the areas where there may be some measure of agreement between our two parties'), highlighting in particular economic strategy and a referendum on electoral reform, where we thought we were at one with the Lib Dems. The statement ended with a restatement of the 'strong, stable and principled' government theme of the night before.

The difficulty was not in deciding the content of the statement but where and how it should be delivered. Should he deliver it in No. 10 as Prime Minister or in Victoria Street as Leader of the Labour Party? Gordon wanted to do it in the state rooms of No. 10 with an autocue. But word came from Gus O'Donnell, by emissary, that he didn't think No. 10 should be used. 'For God's sake, you're still Prime Minister and speaking as such,' said Alastair, 'you're not fleeing to no man's land.' As a compromise, it was decided to make the statement in Downing Street from a lectern. This was also to be the format of his subsequent statements on Monday and Tuesday.

But the press office could not find a suitably mobile lectern. 'Are you sure you need one?' asked Sue Nye. 'Yes, this is too important to do from memory,' said Gordon. After another hunt, a rickety old lectern was found, which had to be taped down outside No. 10 to keep it stable.

The statement, delivered at 1.40 p.m. against the background whirring of the TV helicopter, came over strongly and kept GB to the fore as Clegg and Cameron took their first steps together. Once delivered, exhaustion set in among the GB team. Some went home to get changed and get a bit of sleep; others fell asleep at their desks.

Gordon took calls on the euro crisis and the election results and considered his pitch to Clegg. And he waited for Cameron.

•••

David Cameron's statement at 2.30 p.m. was a thunderbolt. Far from proclaiming victory and demanding the keys to No. 10 immediately, he declared – three times – his intention to make 'a big, open and comprehensive offer to the Liberal Democrats'. Directly pitching for a coalition, he described a minority Conservative government as 'one option' but emphasised the 'common ground' between the Tory and Lib Dem manifestos. 'There is a case for going further than an arrangement which simply keeps a minority Conservative government in office,' he said. 'I want us to work together in tackling our country's big and urgent problems ... I think we have a strong basis for a strong government.' Like Gordon, he mentioned electoral reform explicitly. He only promised a committee of inquiry to look at the issue but was quick to add: 'Inevitably the negotiations we are about to start will involve compromise.'

Gordon's first reaction was that Cameron had made a strategic error. 'He's underestimated his strength and legitimised the whole process of talks and negotiations,' he said as he watched in the war room. Our hope was that this process would turn to our favour once the Tories and Lib Dems had rehearsed the extent of their differences. It also removed any lingering question of GB resigning immediately. The Queen's Private Secretary, Christopher Geidt, was consistently clear throughout the five days that Gordon Brown should remain in office while credible talks between the parties were continuing, and there was no pressure from the other parties for him to do otherwise. The Queen herself spent the weekend at Windsor Castle as normal, although the significance of this was not noticed beyond royal circles at the time.

Cameron had made a strategic error if there was, indeed, no meeting of minds with Clegg. However, the post-statement moves between the Tories and the Lib Dems were swift and positive: an afternoon phone conversation between the leaders briefed as having gone well, and two hours of high-level talks between negotiators of the two parties in the Cabinet Office in the evening. Comprising William Hague, George Osborne and Oliver Letwin, the Tory team could not have been more heavyweight.

On our side, the initial moves were tentative and uncertain. Peter had a further phone conversation with Danny Alexander at 3.30. Danny reiterated Nick Clegg's commitment to a 'twin-track' process, with Lab–Lib discussions to follow the initial Tory discussions. A call between Clegg and GB was fixed for 5 p.m. The big obstacles were also broached directly for the first time. 'Nick views Gordon with great suspicion,' Danny said bluntly. 'A government headed by Gordon Brown, who has been defeated, would be difficult.'

•••

The 5 p.m. Clegg–Brown call was the first contact between them since the election.

After congratulations from GB on Clegg's campaign and results ('rather like an uncle congratulating a nephew on good exam results', one No. 10 aide recalled with a wince), they each sought to make one key point and kept coming back to it. Nick's key point to Gordon was about process: talks with Labour would take place after those with the Tories, which had yet to become substantive, so there couldn't be any immediate Lib–Lab negotiations. 'I've only got this one negotiating team, and they can't talk to both sides at the same time.' Gordon's point to Nick was about the common ground on policy between the parties and how he believed they could co-operate. 'I've been reading your manifesto and I've written two papers on your policy positions and how we can work together. I can get them to you tonight if you like.' Nick seemed surprised at this but said, 'I'd really like to see your note.' Gordon then went through the main policy areas – electoral reform, tax, the deficit, Europe – 'I really think we can work together on all this.' Clegg reiterated that he'd really like to see GB's note.

As the conversation was ending, Gordon changed tack. 'There are some things I need to say to you face to face, if we can meet tomorrow.' Those listening to the call in the war room (GB was in his inner office) knew this was about his personal position and exchanged glances. Nick agreed but said he had a meeting with his MPs and his party executive during the day. 'I'll get back to you if that's OK,' he said about arrangements.

It had been civil and workmanlike. GB was the *demandeur*, doing the pushing. At a few points he talked over Clegg, 'a bit like LBJ [the US President] on the tapes, holding the receiver close, exuding urgency, as GB always does on the phone', as an aide put it. But there were no unpleasant, let alone angry, exchanges. Those listening in No. 10 thought it had been a constructive first move. The concern was to get the policy papers in shape to send to the Lib Dems that evening; they had only been written for internal consumption.

•••

Other phone calls on Friday evening were less constructive. Tony Blair had been speaking to his former inner circle, including some senior ministers and ex-ministers, calling it a 'serious error' for Gordon and Labour to be trying to stay in office. 'The Tories may not have won the election but we lost it,' was his line.

One of his inner circle was blunter still. 'We are in danger of destroying the Labour Party for ever. This approach is madness,' ran the text to me.

•••

And unbeknown to Gordon Brown or his team, another critical conversation was being prepared for Saturday morning.

A key member of Clegg's team was gearing up to tell the BBC that Nick's phone call with Gordon Brown had gone extremely badly, in marked contrast to the pleasant and positive tone of the conversation with David Cameron.

SATURDAY 8 MAY

'**S**witch', the collective name for No. 10's super-efficient switchboard operators who can track virtually anyone down anywhere, was at work on the Prime Minister's calls from 7 a.m. Why had the policy note intended for Clegg still not gone over? Was the first meeting fixed yet with the Lib Dem negotiators? Should he go to Scotland overnight, as Ed Balls was suggesting? Gordon's twin concerns were to counter any impression of 'clinging to power' while kick-starting formal talks with the Lib Dems precisely to keep Labour in power.

The policy note was emailed to Clegg's office first thing. Peter Mandelson and Danny Alexander agreed that Lib Dem and Labour negotiating teams would meet for an initial session in the afternoon.

The Lib Dems planned to assemble the same team as met the Tories the night before – Danny, David Laws, Chris Huhne and Andrew Stunell, the party's former Chief Whip. We debated who to field. There would be Peter and myself, for our negotiating proximity to both GB and the Lib Dems. Gordon decided on the two Eds – Miliband and Balls – as the other two, to underline his personal commitment and to demonstrate support across the Cabinet and party. Ed Balls was in his Yorkshire constituency home and agreed to drive down to London.

During the morning, the No. 10 policy team worked up options for an electoral reform referendum. Gordon was attracted to holding it as soon as the autumn (of 2010). We discussed making it a broader 'political reform' referendum, including questions on an elected House of Lords and banning MPs from taking second paid jobs.

The official advice was that for technical and legislative reasons, a referendum could not be held before May 2011 at the earliest. I pushed back strongly, and drew up plans for a referendum by November (2010) at the latest. In 1997, devolution to Scotland and Wales was carried swiftly on the back of successful referendums held barely four months after the general election. The Labour government in the 1970s made the mistake of delaying devolution referendums until late in its term, when they simply became votes on the government's unpopularity. Also, an early referendum would glue the coalition together as a united progressive force. Within weeks Lib Dem and Labour ministers would be campaigning shoulder to shoulder in support of the Alternative Vote, even if different positions were taken on full proportional representation. A successful referendum would give the government popular legitimacy as a coalition, and a new lease of life.

•••

Should Gordon go to Scotland? The idea was for Gordon and family to leave after the Cenotaph ceremony at noon for the 65th anniversary of VE Day, at which he would be laying a wreath alongside the Prince of Wales.

Gordon was concerned this would make it harder to engage with Nick Clegg. 'We need to meet tonight; it's got to be today. If there isn't serious progress by Monday morning when the markets open, a panic will be on and the Tories will be in.' This last concern was heightened by a conversation with Shriti Vadera, his former economic adviser, who warned of possible market meltdown on Monday morning if by then there wasn't a new government or signs of one imminently.

Then someone showed Gordon *The Sun*'s front page banner headline: 'SQUATTER, 59, HOLED UP IN NO. 10', next to an unflattering mugshot. 'A man aged fifty-nine was squatting in a luxury home near the Houses of Parliament last night...' ran the story.

'There will be loads more of that tomorrow,' said Alastair Campbell.

'OK, we're going to Scotland,' Gordon decided. The Cenotaph ceremony, at which Clegg and Cameron were also to be present, would give the chance for a private word with Clegg, and a meeting could be fixed for Sunday once the first round of discussions between the two parties' negotiators had taken place. The plan was to return on Sunday morning.

Clegg was in any case in meetings of his party's MPs and executive for most of Saturday afternoon and evening. The Lib Dems in Soviet-style constant session, seemingly at all hours of day and night, was an abiding feature of the five days, to the mounting irritation of some Labour MPs who only knew what the TV news told them about what was going on. GB and his staff kept senior ministers in touch by phone over the weekend, but he did not want to summon Labour MPs to a meeting until talks had made progress and there was real momentum towards a coalition, in order to minimise opposition. By the end of the weekend this was causing tension with the officers of the Parliamentary Labour Party (PLP). On Monday it was agreed with PLP chair Tony Lloyd to summon the full PLP for Wednesday, which turned out to be after GB's resignation.

As GB was in his inner office tying a black tie for the Cenotaph ceremony, talks with the Lib Dems almost derailed before they had even begun.

Just after 11.30 a.m., a breathless Jon Sopel reported on his daily BBC1 election programme that he had been briefed 'by a very senior Lib Dem source who is close to the negotiations' that a phone call had taken place between Brown and Clegg the previous evening and that the conversation had been 'pretty terrible'. Sopel reported that his Lib Dem source 'said it was a diatribe, a rant, and that Gordon Brown was threatening in his approach to Nick Clegg and that Nick Clegg came off the phone at the end of it feeling that while politically the Labour Party and the Lib Dems may not be that far apart, actually the person in the shape of Gordon Brown would be someone it would be impossible to enter into a partnership with because of his general attitude in working with other people'.

There was immediate astonishment and anger in the war room. It had been agreed by both sides that the Clegg–Brown call would not be briefed, so this sounded to us like a deliberate Lib Dem hatchet job. But why? Whatever view Clegg might have of Brown, and however animated Gordon may have been on the phone, it was not remotely true to describe the call as bad, let alone a 'diatribe' or 'rant'. Assuming this wasn't a freelance operation, it could only have one of two purposes. Either to undermine all prospect of Lib–Lab talks. Or to undermine Gordon and engineer his removal as the prelude to any talks.

Peter Mandelson got on to Jon Sopel immediately. Jon told him the briefing had come 'straight from one of Nick Clegg's right-hand men'. (This was true: it turned out to have been Paddy Ashdown.)

Ever quick to spot the chink in the armour, Peter responded: 'You mean it came from just one source. You broadcast this broadside on the basis of just one source? Aren't you supposed to have more than one source?' The story was total and utter nonsense, he went on, and had to be corrected immediately. 'Jon, you are a dear friend but someone is making you out to be a right nana,' he ended, with a characteristic hint of menace.

Clegg's office immediately told us that they knew nothing of the briefing and it had been unauthorised. GB was nonplussed. If it was unauthorised, why had Sopel taken it so seriously? 'Perhaps because it was intended to be taken so seriously,' said Alastair, pointing out the obvious.

But there was no time to ruminate; mobiles were exploding

with journalists wanting confirmation and comment. Peter got on to Danny Alexander. They agreed that both sides would say the Clegg–Brown phone call had been 'amiable' and the Sopel story 'entirely without foundation'. Iain Bundred, GB's spokesman, and Jonny Oates, his Lib Dem counterpart, briefed this out, while calls were made to Nick Robinson, Laura Kuenssberg, and other BBC reporters, hammering home the 'only one source' point to limit the damage.

This largely succeeded in stopping the story as a running news item. It nonetheless became the received wisdom that while Clegg and Cameron were getting on really well, their every conversation forging a closer bond and rapport, the opposite was true of the Clegg–Brown encounters.

•••

While Gordon left for the Cenotaph, his team stayed in the war room debating next steps. To meet concern about the markets and media demanding a new government by Monday morning, and to encourage the Lib Dems to proceed with greater urgency, we drafted a further GB statement setting out his duty to ensure there was not 'a protracted period of uncertainty' and his 'firm view that a conclusion [to inter-party talks] needs to be reached by Tuesday morning'. 'At this point it will be clear how the next government will be formed and I will act accordingly in the advice I submit to HM the Queen,' ran the draft.

The idea was that by setting Tuesday as the deadline, this

would calm the markets and gain Monday as a negotiating day while making clear to the Lib Dems that this was
the limit. We discussed whether to go further and say that
GB would also resign on Tuesday if the Lib Dems had still
not indicated which side they would support, advising the
Queen to send for Cameron to form a government as leader
of the largest party. Peter was against this because it might
exacerbate the uncertainty we were seeking to reduce.

As early as Saturday morning none of us – politicians, advisers or civil servants – thought the negotiating period could
be extended beyond Tuesday. This might be only five days
after the election result, a fraction of the period customarily
taken by Continental politicians to negotiate post-election
coalitions, but expectations were different in their political
systems. Media expectations of a new or re-elected Prime
Minister being in No. 10 on the Friday morning after the
election were too great, despite Sir Gus O'Donnell's Cabinet
Office guidance and the objective fact that complex negotiations had to take place between the political parties before
any coalition could conceivably be put together.

But it wasn't just media expectations. It was also human
endurance. Because the drama of negotiations started within
hours of an election night when no one had got much sleep,
and was expected to continue non-stop until there was an
outcome, exhaustion bred exhaustion. For those of us in the
thick of it, the nights barely existed. And there was an escalat-
ing sense of No. 10 under siege. By now every entrance leading
to No. 10 – including those on Whitehall and Horse Guards,
which the media had not previously doorstepped – was

swarming with a steadily larger mass of jostling cameras and journalists, greater by far than ever experienced in the past by any of us in No. 10. Simply getting in and out of the building became an ordeal. Media helicopters were constantly whirring overhead – 'more choppers than for the O. J. Simpson trial', one aide quipped as we struggled to converse above the din in the No. 10 garden. By Tuesday this had all become almost unbearable.

•••

GB returned from the Cenotaph with discussion on the proposed statement in mid-flow. 'They've already started the transfer of power,' he joked, relating a last-minute change of proceedings at the Cenotaph. Instead of the Prime Minister laying a wreath alongside Prince Charles, as had been the plan, all three party leaders were given wreaths. At the rather stilted reception afterwards, Sir David Richards, the Chief of the General Staff, told Gordon that his greatest achievement would be keeping Britain out of the euro. 'So they've started writing my obituary too.'

Gordon said he had caught a word with Nick Clegg after the reception. He went through 'the numbers' with him. 'The arithmetic does work, this is possible,' he had assured Clegg. 'The other parties will support us or abstain.' He explained that this meant a Queen's Speech majority in the mid- to high twenties, which was a surprise to Clegg, who hadn't thought through what the other parties would actually do on the Queen's Speech and subsequent key votes.

'He seemed to register all this carefully, but we didn't have time to go into any detail,' GB reported. Clegg had said his people were looking seriously at the policy paper and they agreed to meet on Sunday.

Gordon looked at the proposed statement while two conversations swirled around. Private secretaries briefed him on the intensifying euro crisis and the EU meetings and discussions planned for the next forty-eight hours. GB needed to take calls and discuss the lines Alistair Darling would be taking. The rest of us tried to finalise the statement and discussed handling of the first negotiating session with the Lib Dems, which had been fixed for 4 p.m. Periodically, Sarah Brown popped her head round the door, warning Gordon of the ever-diminishing time before they absolutely had to leave at 2.30 p.m. for the airport.

Into this scene, Harriet Harman arrived through the front door of No. 10, every camera trained on her. Rather than add yet another person to the drafting committee, Gordon took Harriet to a separate office to brief her. They discussed Labour's negotiating position with the Lib Dems and the proposal to offer them an early referendum on the Alternative Vote, with an additional question on full proportional representation if they so wished but which Labour would not support as a party. Harriet was content with this. 'If we can keep the Tories out with a referendum on AV that's fine by me, and I'm sure the party will be fine, but we can't promise PR,' was her reaction.

Harriet's bigger concern was that she had been asked to go on *The Andrew Marr Show* on Sunday morning and really wanted to do it, but she had been told that Gordon and his media team didn't want ministers on *Marr* or other programmes for fear they might cause difficulties with the negotiations. After much to-ing and fro-ing she agreed, reluctantly, to come off *Marr* if no other minister was doing Sunday interviews either. This involved No. 10 phoning round the entire Cabinet on Saturday afternoon, with Peter doing the more sensitive calls. Everyone agreed.

By the time Gordon finished with Harriet, he absolutely had to leave for Scotland. The statement was left in limbo. It was decided simply to brief the line about GB's concern being to ensure there was not a 'protracted period of uncertainty', with an outcome likely by 'the middle of next week', in order to calm the markets. This carried through into the rest of the day's media and into Sunday.

The 24-hour news channels anyway had a good running story in a noisy demonstration for electoral reform and against a Lib Dem deal with the Tories outside the meeting of Lib Dem MPs taking place in Transport House in Smith Square. This 'spontaneous' demo – awash with 'Fair Votes Now' and 'Stand Up and Be Counted' placards – was anything but. It had been pre-planned by a group of young Labour activists more than a week previously for precisely the post-election scenario now unfolding. The same organisation got an anti-Tory petition delivered to Cowley Street and thousands of emails flooding into the Lib Dems urging them to keep clear of the Tories. Lib Dem donors were also targeted.

If the idea was to unsettle the Lib Dems, it appeared to

have that effect. 'Don't do a deal with them, don't do a deal with them,' pleaded the good natured protesters, cameras by their side, as Simon Hughes and other MPs left the building. Following chants of 'We Want Nick', Clegg emerged from the building to address the protesters. 'Take it from me, reforming politics is one of the reasons I went into politics,' he shouted into the loudspeaker, as GB's plane to Edinburgh waited to take off.

As for most of the five days, David Cameron was nowhere to be seen.

•••

With GB on his way to the airport, his team took stock. We all felt a sense of drift. Engagement was cranking up with the Lib Dems, and the principle of a progressive coalition was strongly supported by most of Gordon's team. But the running was being made by the Tories, and Clegg clearly wanted this to be the case. Unless this changed by the end of the weekend, the game was surely over, and staying in office for even a day longer would be humiliating and damaging to Labour's standing and unity.

Then there was the issue of GB's own leadership; none of us knew how this would be resolved. There was also positive relish in some quarters at the idea of a Tory government supported by the Lib Dems embarking on the mother of all public spending cuts, while Labour reaped the political whirlwind to follow. Alastair worried out loud that Gordon was being 'tactical rather than strategic' and Tony's concerns and views were being regularly reported to me and others of his former staff in No. 10.

Straightforward dissent was bubbling up elsewhere. David Blunkett, who had called the election for the Tories shortly after the exit poll on election night, was now agitating for Cameron simply to be allowed to take office. 'We've lost; they've basically won; that's all there is to it,' was his message. He also had no time for the Lib Dems, Sheffield being a fierce Lab–Lib battleground both in council and parliamentary elections. GB and Blunkett exchanged voice-mail messages; Blunkett agreed not to go 'OTT' in media appearances, but he did not modify his view. Siobhain McDonagh and John Mann were among MPs taking the same line. Within the Cabinet, Jack Straw and Andy Burnham were in a similar place and told Gordon so on the phone.

However, this was a minority view in the higher reaches of the party. In phone calls on Thursday evening and Friday, the leaders of the biggest trade unions had all been squared by GB in support of a 'progressive coalition' to keep the Tories out. (Tony Woodley of Unite could not be contacted at first; he was in Cuba.) GB saw trade union support as critical if and when it came to a decision for coalition. Almost all Cabinet ministers contacted in the Saturday ring-round, and in conversations with GB personally, were supportive or not hostile. A number, including Alan Johnson, Ben Bradshaw and Peter Hain, were ardent enthusiasts for Lab–Libbery and electoral reform. The crucial swing figure was David Miliband. Once David grasped 'the numbers', he was content to proceed. But everything depended upon whether the Lib Dems ultimately wanted to govern with us rather than the Tories. This is what we were about to explore properly with them for the first time.

•••

Danny Alexander was insistent that the first meeting between our two negotiating teams, set for 4 p.m. in an hour between different internal Lib Dem party meetings, should be private and informal with no civil servants present. It therefore could not be held under the gaze of the waiting media in the Cabinet Office building at 70 Whitehall, where the Lib Dems had met the Tories the evening before. He suggested instead Portcullis House, the new parliamentary building opposite the Houses of Parliament at the top of Whitehall, which would be deserted on a Saturday afternoon.

So at 3.45 p.m., Peter, Ed Miliband, Gavin Kelly and I walked through to the basement of the Cabinet Office to be driven in Peter's Jag, which was parked there, across Whitehall to the Norman Shaw block of parliamentary offices. From here we took the back entrance to Portcullis House, hoping this indirect route would avoid any journalists tracking us to our destination. We also weren't sure that Portcullis House would be open on the first Saturday afternoon after the election, and we might need a custodian to take us through.

We didn't, but the large atrium plaza of Portcullis House was spookily deserted save for one coffee counter with a single member of staff in the far corner. Ed Balls was there, and shouted for us to come and join him. 'I need some money to pay for my coffee,' he said. 'When I stopped at a service station on the motorway I found I'd left without my wallet. Yvette had to phone through my credit card number to buy the petrol.' I gave him £20 and he bought us all coffees.

We took the lift up to a third-floor conference room overlooking Big Ben and waited for the Lib Dems, who had still to materialise, apart from Tim Snowball, Nick Clegg's assistant. A few minutes later three of their team – Danny, Chris Huhne and Andrew Stunell – arrived ('Sorry, we had to dodge all those fair votes protesters,' said Danny). David Laws was another twenty minutes late, by when the meeting was well underway.

Sitting opposite us around the large round conference table, Danny opened. 'We are keen to hear what you have to say to us, both about policy and the viability of any arrangement. We are essentially in listening mode. As you know, the Conservatives have put proposals to us, and we want to hear what you have to say.'

Copies of the note we had sent over in the morning were circulated. Peter began by setting out 'the numbers', courtesy of a sheet in front of him laying them all out. There was a short discussion of the various Northern Ireland parties; the Lib Dems seemed unaware of the degree of animosity between the DUP and the Tories, and why it was therefore likely the DUP would support a Lab–Lib coalition without the need for any formal deal. We agreed there could be no Ulster sectarianism behind any coalition.

The discussion moved on to three of the headings in the policy note: political reform, tax and spending, and home affairs. The timing and content of an electoral reform referendum was the first issue. I set out our thinking on a quick referendum. Chris Huhne said they would need a larger 'down payment' – 'down payment' was to be a Lib Dem mantra in all our discussions on electoral reform – than simply a referendum; they needed the full AV electoral system enacted in immediate legislation too, even before the referendum.

Ed Miliband observed: 'Why do you need this? Either you believe in the power of your argument for the referendum or you don't.' 'Our activists simply won't believe you are serious unless we get this down payment,' said Chris.

Chris, however, immediately went on to say that the Tory offer of a committee to discuss electoral reform was 'a joke', and our support for AV was 'a decisive issue' for them. The only edge to this part of the discussion was an exchange on the Wright Committee's report on the handling of House of Commons business. Andrew Stunell asked if we would agree to Wright's proposal that the timetabling of government business in the House of Commons be passed to a new committee elected by the House itself. Peter, who like the rest of us had barely heard of the Wright Committee, said we would happily consider this but needed to be careful about creating 'a rod for our own backs' by losing control of government business in the Commons.

'That shows the difference between us,' said Stunell tartly. 'We want to end the elective dictatorship; for you it is second nature. We are about real change and want to give power away.'

'Elective dictatorship?' said Peter quizzically. 'I haven't noticed too much of that in recent years.'

On tax-and-spend, a discussion led by David Laws focused on the Lib Dem proposal that there could and should be immediate in-year spending cuts for 2010/11 and 'further and faster' spending cuts than Labour's plans thereafter. There was also discussion of two particular Lib Dem spending proposals: a new £2.5 billion 'pupil premium' for disadvantaged school pupils, and raising the tax threshold to £10,000 at a cost of £17 billion. Chris Huhne said that immediate cuts were now possible without jeopardising the recovery because the depreciation of sterling in recent weeks 'has provided a large, real, extra stimulus to the economy'.

On 'further and faster' cuts beyond 2010/11, Ed Balls raised the credibility of a coalition government claiming it would cut the deficit while pushing ahead with costly new tax-and-spend proposals. 'There is an important academic article about this, by Alesina and Ardagna, which says that coalitions don't have the credibility of single-party govern-ments on deficit reduction, so we need to be really careful not to make unrealistic statements on tax and spending.'

Chris Huhne, also a heavy-duty economist, played snap: 'I've read Alesina and Ardagna too, and it's not as simple as that, Ed – they also say that the creation of a new govern-ment is when you can act decisively on debt – and that's what we are doing.'

'Well, no one can say we aren't acting decisively,' countered Ed. 'But if you want to cut more while also spending more, that's the difficulty.'

The rest of us had never heard of Alesina or Ardagna, so let this one run. Also, no figures were offered by Chris or David as to the scale of the 'further and faster' cuts they had in mind. Given the draconian deficit reduction already planned by Alistair Darling, and the scale of the extra Lib Dem spending, we assumed this was rhetorical flourish.

The discussion moved on to various items in the Lib Dems' proposed 'Freedom Bill', particularly the abolition of identity cards and a more restrictive approach to retaining DNA on the DNA database. I indicated that we were prepared to consider all this.

It was coming up to 5 p.m. and the Lib Dems needed to leave for their party executive meeting.

'Any other issues for now?' asked Danny, who was effectively in the chair.

'Yes, Gordon Brown and your leadership,' said Chris Huhne. 'This is the biggest issue for us…'

He was immediately cut dead by Danny. 'No, Chris, no. This is not for you to raise. Absolutely not. It's a matter for the leaders themselves and we are not discussing it here.'

Stunell then asked bluntly how serious we were about delivering and what guarantees we could give. Peter passed this on to me. I said this was why we were intent on a coalition and a project – including an early referendum – which absolutely bound us together to deliver. Heads nodded on all sides. On that note we ended, with handshakes all round,

Peter and Danny agreeing to speak later about next moves. The Lib Dems left the room while we remained.

After a few seconds' silence, Ed M piped up: 'I hate to say it, but I think this is destined to succeed. There wasn't anything big on which we disagreed, assuming they don't mean that stuff about faster cuts.' We all expressed cautious optimism. The discussion had been easy and constructive, with no obvious show-stoppers, and mutual agreement to reflect on the points raised. Only Andrew Stunell, a wiry, persistent man, had irritated Peter with his aggressive point-making and mini-lecture on the elective dictatorship. 'Who is he? He looks like one of those classic pavement Liberals. I've never ever seen him before – why did they bring him?' The two Eds said they had never come across him either. I said he was an ex-local-government leader and had a reputa-tion in the Lib Dems as an expert in coalition-mongering in hung local authorities, which was presumably why he was on the team.

It was agreed that Gavin, who had been taking notes, would prepare an updated list of issues to be addressed at the next meeting. Ed Balls then left to drive back up to Yorkshire. The rest of us went back to Downing Street to call GB and to brief officials, then home, agreeing to gather in the war room at about ten on Sunday morning.

In retrospect, the most significant aspect of this first nego-tiating session is what did not happen. It was not briefed by the Lib Dems afterwards – either to the media or to their party colleagues – as having gone badly, unlike the subsequent two Lib–Lab negotiating sessions. In fact, it was not briefed at all. As for the report back to colleagues, this must have been positive because in a call on Sunday, Paddy Ashdown told me it had been 'inspired' to include Ed Balls in our team as it demonstrated the seriousness with which we were taking the talks. Danny Alexander was evidently of the same view. Later in the evening he texted me asking for Ed's mobile number.

•••

There was, however, briefing taking place on other fronts. Later in the evening came a text came from a friend in the higher reaches of News International: 'So it looks like a deal will be in place tomorrow, ready to put to the two parties' members on Monday. Cameron had a very good seventy-minute meeting with Clegg tonight. He's having to make more concessions to deliver Lib Dems but nothing that will be a real deal-breaker.'

'The end is nigh,' one of Gordon's media aides emailed. 'There is very strong Tory and Lib Dem briefing that a deal will be done in the next few days.'

I phoned GB in Scotland to tell him this. He was about to talk to Clegg again on the phone. We discussed next moves. The crucial thing was the first face-to-face meeting the following day. We went, yet again, through options on electoral reform, the economy and other policy. But, I added, pointing out the obvious: 'This isn't just about policy. He is clearly getting on like a house on fire with Cameron. You need the same rapport.' 'I know, I know,' said GB. 'I'm convinced we can do this. We basically agree on policy and on the whole progressive project. This is the moment to bring it alive. It would be madness for him to go in with the Tories, where none of this is true.'

I had going through my mind one of Nick Clegg's party pieces, told to me earlier in the day by a senior journalist – a fraught meeting at the height of the MPs' expenses crisis in May 2009 between Clegg, GB, Cameron and the then Speaker Michael Martin. Clegg tells it as a complete train-wreck, with GB 'hectoring' him and Cameron to agree proposals he had already set out in public, ending with Clegg saying there was no point in the discussion continuing, and he and Cameron leaving together and agreeing, exasperated, that they couldn't do business with Brown. As was becoming increasingly clear on that Saturday evening, however, Clegg and Cameron could do business with each other.

Gordon had not cultivated Nick Clegg before the election. They barely knew each other outside formal exchanges in the House of Commons. He had placed greater store by his relations with other senior Lib Dems. He had a good relationship with Ming Campbell, not just as near constituency neighbours but in terms of age and Lib–Lab outlook. When Ming was Lib Dem leader they even discussed issuing a joint statement of principles and objectives to build a common front at the coming general election, before Ming's leadership collapsed in favour of Clegg.

Gordon also had a strong rapport with Vince Cable, again not just in terms of age and Scottish politics, but a political association going back to the 1970s when both were

up-and-coming Scottish Labour figures, Vince as a Glasgow
Labour councillor and contributor to GB's 1975 'Red Paper
on Scotland'. Vince had twice been GB's guest in No. 10,
once with his wife. A gem of a story told by GB's aides is of
one of these visits, shortly before the June 2009 reshuffle.
After drinks in the No. 10 flat, Gordon gave Vince a tour of
the building, ending with the two walking together into the
war room in animated friendly conversation. Ed Balls had
arrived in the war room shortly before; when he beheld the
entry of Gordon and Vince – Chancellor Vince? – 'his jaw
dropped and his face was a joy to behold', goes the tale.

GB phoned Ming and Vince personally on Sunday,
Monday and Tuesday. But Nick Clegg was the linchpin, and
that rapport had still to be built.

The Saturday-evening call between them was another
step forward. Nick (according to Gordon's later account)
summarised the state of play with the Tories. He and David
Cameron had spoken and their parties' negotiators were to
have a second session at 11 a.m. the next morning. But he
wanted to intensify the dialogue with Labour. Gordon went
through 'the numbers' in more detail than had been possible
after the Cenotaph. Nick queried reliance on DUP, as had his
negotiators at the earlier meeting, and GB assured him that
it wasn't necessary to have any formal arrangement. Nick
said he understood now that the parliamentary arithmetic
could make for a viable Lab–Lib coalition. (Paddy Ashdown
was saying the same to Labour friends on Saturday, so this
message was getting through.)

Nick said, diplomatically, that there were obviously other

factors crucial to the government being seen as fresh and legitimate, while GB emphasised the economic crisis afoot, talked about the possibility of a joint statement and the need for real progress in any talks to be evident by Monday. They agreed that the meeting of the two teams had been a good first session, and agreed to meet personally in the early afternoon of the Sunday. Again, GB's own position was not discussed directly.

Aides immediately set about identifying a time and venue for the meeting. Four p.m., at the home of a Lib Dem peer in Regent's Park, was agreed upon.

•••

Lab–Lib engagement was notching up a gear. But it didn't take Chris Huhne's blunt intervention in the first Lib–Lab talks to identify the elephant in the room – Gordon's own position.

Late on Saturday morning, Gordon's aide Stewart Wood walked over to Peter Mandelson in the war room to ask him about something. Peter was texting. As Stewart looked over his shoulder he saw a message about to be sent to Danny Alexander. It was a simple question: 'How much of an obstacle to a deal is Gordon for Nick?'

We were about to find out.

SUNDAY 9 MAY

The only people in the war room as I arrived at 10 a.m. on Sunday morning were Gordon's policy advisers Gavin Kelly, Matt Cavanagh and Nick Pearce, plus Nick Pearce's toddler son, Hal. 'Who knows, he could be Prime Minister by this evening,' quipped Gavin, as Hal raced around between the desks.

The four of us adults spent the next few hours delving into the policy issues for the next negotiating session with the Lib Dems. This had been tentatively scheduled for 6.30 p.m., after the Clegg–GB meeting and the second negotiating session between the Lib Dems and the Tories, due to start at 11 a.m.

Gordon had emailed overnight with a plan on how to get to the Lib Dems' £10,000 tax threshold in stages over a parliament, starting with pensioners. We were also deciding how much ground we could give on Home Office issues in particular. Abandoning ID cards wasn't a particular problem; they were now voluntary and Alan Johnson was not wedded to them except for foreign nationals. The scope of the DNA database and biometric passports were also negotiable, but not, we thought, renegotiation of the entire extradition treaty with the United States, which also featured in the Lib Dem 'Freedom Bill'.

The war room filled up as the morning wore on. Peter dropped by. Together with aides who had been phoning round, he went through the stance of all members of the Cabinet in preparation for calls GB was planning to make in the afternoon. Peter then decamped through the connecting door from No. 10 to the Cabinet Office and a grand, empty suite of rooms overlooking Horse Guards Parade – soon to become Nick Clegg's offices as Deputy Prime Minister – where he was often to be found during the next two days stretched out on a large white couch, Blackberrying away in front of Sky or BBC News 24, sometimes messaging the journalists on the TV in front of him. Alastair popped in and out too as we awaited Gordon's return, punctuated by phone calls from Gordon in the car from the airport.

•••

We couldn't make up our collective mind whether the Lib Dems were talking to us for real or for show. Cameron and Clegg had held a long meeting in Admiralty House the previous evening which both sides were briefing positively. But then the Lib Dems were also briefing the second Clegg–Brown call, the previous evening, as 'amicable'.

Paddy Ashdown's performance on *The Andrew Marr Show* was especially perplexing. Paddy was the Lib Dems' main talking head and carried weight both with Clegg and with

David Laws, who seemed to us the pivotal Lib Dem figure in the negotiations. From calls to various of us, Paddy now appeared to understand 'the numbers' and was warming to a Lab–Lib coalition. But on *Marr*, he leaned decisively the other way. 'The British electorate have invented an exquisite method of torture for the Lib Dems; our instincts go one way, the mathematics go the other,' he said, adding: 'I admire the way the Conservative Party has responded … I think Mr Cameron has shown a certain degree of leadership.' He was also openly sceptical about a 'panjandrum alliance' against the Tories ('Would that provide the kind of government capable of taking strong decisions? … The answer seems to me self-evident … There may be other ways round it … I don't know.') He was also brutally dismissive of GB:

'Amongst his personal qualities, it seems to me, is not one that makes him an easy or a very able leader of a collegiate-style government. Now that's a question for Gordon.'

However, barely out of the BBC studio, Paddy was phoning Labour friends to make clear that he had not meant any slight to Gordon. He had definitely not closed the door to a possible Lab–Lib deal, and could this be made clear to Gordon personally.

•••

Gordon arrived back in No. 10 at about 1 p.m. and launched into phone calls with Cabinet colleagues and discussions on policy positions in preparation for the Clegg meeting.

He also called Mervyn King, the Governor of the Bank of England, worried at reports that the Bank had been in contact with George Osborne and the Lib Dems urging the need for a bigger and faster cuts programme.

In the midst of this, the Queen's Private Secretary, Christopher Geidt, appeared in person, as he did again on Monday, dapper and discreet, to be briefed by the Prime Minister on the state of play. The Palace was content with the inter-party negotiation process, and didn't want anything precipitate to happen before there was a clear outcome.

The venue for the Clegg–Brown meeting was changed to the Foreign Office. There was no way that the two leaders were going to get to Regent's Park, as previously planned, without the entire press corps and helicopters following them there and back.

Even reaching the Foreign Office unnoticed proved impossible. Slipping out of the ground-floor French windows into the Horse Guards Road rear courtyard of No. 10 shortly after 4 p.m., Gordon walked briskly the few yards across to the rear private entrance of the Foreign Office. A television producer by the side of St James's Park spotted him and moments later was on the phone to Iain Bundred asking if GB was going to a meeting with Clegg. Iain said he couldn't give a running commentary on GB's movements; there were plenty of reasons he could have walked across to the Foreign Office, including its excellent Costa Coffee which was better than anything in No. 10. But mobiles promptly exploded again. Iain and Jonny Oates in Clegg's office set to work on media lines to put out after the meeting.

•••

The meeting was in Permanent Secretary Sir Peter Ricketts's grand office. Sir Peter Ricketts was there to welcome the two leaders in person. 'You want it to be known as the Ricketts accord,' quipped a Private Secretary as Clegg and Brown went in alone for the best part of eighty minutes.

According to GB's later account to me, Nick Clegg said he would definitely make a decision one way or another between the Tories or Labour. He would not sit on the fence, and he was determined only to support a progressive pro-European government. (Europe was a key issue in many of the Brown–Clegg discussions and often appeared to be of greatest concern to Nick personally.) He said his preference was for a coalition, not a looser arrangement, because otherwise it was bound to collapse and the Lib Dems would be wiped out in the subsequent election. But he hadn't as yet decided which party to support. There were still 'serious problems' about working with the Tories. On policy, he thought he was closer to Labour, but there were 'legitimacy' issues about a deal with Labour and with GB personally.

Gordon wanted Nick to understand the depth of his commitment to progressive politics and to working in partnership. 'You have got me completely wrong if you think I'm a tribal politician,' he said. He told him about his pre-election plan for Labour to stand down unilaterally in thirty seats in favour of the Lib Dems, and that he had made his decisive moves on electoral reform in part to make a Lib–Lab arrangement possible.

They ranged across the major policy issues – political reform, the economy, civil liberties and Europe – and then onto the shape of a coalition and how its legitimacy could be underpinned. GB said he was thinking in terms of 'five or six big jobs' for Lib Dems in a coalition, and mentioned Cable, Laws, Ashdown and Huhne as obvious other candidates. Was Clegg interested in a major department himself? 'I don't want to run before I can walk,' was his reply, adding that he would have to pay special attention to constitutional reform since this was the central issue for most Lib Dems.

On legitimacy, GB said that they needed to carry out a nationwide grassroots campaign in favour of the coalition agreement, leading up to the AV referendum which both parties would support. He was attracted to an early referendum; Clegg was too, if there was a 'down payment' of reform in advance of it.

Then they got on to GB's leadership. Gordon said he was 'relaxed' about his own position. He recognised that 'a fresh government needs fresh leadership' and he said he never intended to stay long into the new parliament in any event. Getting political reform and the economic crisis sorted were his remaining tasks. But it wasn't possible to form a coalition government without him. If he, Gordon, resigned, Cameron would be sent for by the Queen, so he had to get the government going. 'Nick never pushed on a timetable and I never gave one,' he recounted. But Nick clearly took this to mean an early departure.

They ended by agreeing to consider further all they had discussed, and to speak again soon, probably later in the day.

There had been one further significant exchange. As they chatted about their backgrounds and what had brought them into politics, Nick remarked: 'I wish we'd had the chance to get to know each other better before.'

...

The meeting seemed to have gone well. GB's aide Justin Forsyth was waiting outside with Tim Snowball from Clegg's office. Towards the end they could hear a good deal of laughter from inside, 'not nervous laughter but genuine laughter', Justin recalled. They came out saying 'all this needs to be sorted', referring to their policy discussions.

There was, however, one immediate bad omen. Iain Bundred and Jonny Oates had agreed a short line for the media about the meeting. The wording was at Jonny's suggestion:

'Following their telephone call last night, Nick Clegg and Gordon Brown met this afternoon at the Foreign Office. Their discussion was amicable.'

Iain walked over to the Foreign Office to clear this line with GB as he left. GB was content. But Jonny rang back to say that Nick wanted it changed to:

'Gordon Brown asked to meet Nick Clegg. Nick Clegg agreed and they had an amicable meeting.'

Jonny was insistent on the change. It was more than a minor change; it put the Clegg–Brown discussions onto a different basis to the Clegg–Cameron discussions, which were briefed as taking place by mutual desire. Back in No. 10,

Gordon was irritated. 'He's worried about Cameron – he doesn't want Cameron thinking he's engaging seriously with us.' After more to-ing and fro-ing, halfway wording was agreed:

'Last night Gordon Brown phoned Nick Clegg. Following their discussion the two met this afternoon at the Foreign Office to update each other. They had an amicable discussion.'

•••

Was Nick Clegg serious? If so, what were the next steps? This was the debate in the war room and in Peter's office for the next two hours. At this point Gordon did not tell even those of us closest to him that he and Nick had discussed his own position explicitly. Since this was a – if not the – critical issue, Peter and I were sceptical there had been a breakthrough.

Furthermore, the Lib Dems were yet again delaying the next round of talks between our negotiating teams, which had been due to take place on the Sunday evening. And their talks with the Tories were still going on in the Cabinet Office. They had been in progress since 11 a.m.; they would hardly be entering their sixth hour if they weren't getting into detail and making reasonable progress. The Tory–Lib Dem meeting did not conclude until 5.30 p.m., with William Hague and Danny Alexander both making statements outside 70 Whitehall saying that they intended to meet again 'within the next twenty-four hours'.

On the other hand, a good deal of policy ground had been covered between GB and Clegg; there appeared to be no deal-breakers; and they had agreed to speak again soon. And the informed media was beginning to think something serious might be afoot. Nick Robinson, who had previously believed a Lib Dem deal with the Tories was a near certainty, texted in mid-afternoon:

'The plan now, I believe, is for Gordon to negotiate deal if possible whilst making clear that he will stand aside at a future point as Tony did. Will you take the initiative or wait for Tory talks to fail?'

'A bit of both…' I texted back.

•••

At around 8 p.m., Danny came back to Peter to say that they would like the next meeting between Nick and Gordon to be very soon indeed.

At 9.35 p.m., barely four hours after their Foreign Office meeting, they met for a further long conversation. This one was not so amicable. The critical issue, which Clegg had clearly been discussing with his inner team, was GB's own position. When would he go, and how would the transition be handled?

After the media circus around the earlier meeting, preparations worthy of a Feydeau farce were made for the two leaders to get to the next meeting unobserved. The venue decided upon was the Prime Minister's room in the heart of the House of Commons, down a short corridor from the Chamber, because it was immediately available and the Commons was bound to be empty late on a Sunday evening. But how to get there? It was decided to go through the tunnel from the Cabinet Office to the Ministry of Defence, which runs under Whitehall; and to walk from there through a back entrance to the Commons. The meeting was also kept secret from the half-dozen of GB's closest aides who had been in No. 10 throughout the weekend. They were told that nothing more would be happening until the morning, so they decamped to the Clarence pub on Whitehall on their way home.

Whereupon the farce continued. GB was spotted walking through the House of Commons with Peter Mandelson by an ITN journalist, who phoned Iain Bundred in the Clarence to ask if another meeting with Clegg was taking place, or was it a meeting of all the party leaders to agree a statement in advance of the markets opening on Monday? Iain said he hadn't the faintest idea why GB had gone over to the Commons, but he, Iain, would hardly be in the pub if it was a crucial meeting. ITN did not report anything.

•••

Gordon thought the idea was for Danny and Peter to join the start of the meeting to discuss the policy agenda and next steps in the negotiations, and then to leave him and Nick alone. But the four of them ended up staying for the whole discussion, and as it moved on to the issue of Gordon's position, Danny became the 'tough cop' to Nick's 'soft cop'.

Nick started by passing Gordon a 'heads of agreement' note on the possible shape of a Lab–Lib accord which his policy team had prepared for the talks intended to take place that evening, but which it was agreed would now take place the following day.

'I have taken everything you said this afternoon to heart,' Nick opened. 'There is a basic affinity of purpose between us. I am excited by the proposition of our two parties being able to deliver change.' He said he was still talking to the Conservatives. 'They have gone far further in their policy offer than before. It doesn't tick all the boxes, there are still some fundamental differences, but it is better than we could have imagined.'

The discussion started on electoral reform and fixed-term parliaments. GB rehearsed the argument for an early referendum. Nick asked about the possibility of immediate legislation on the Alternative Vote and said they would probably want an option or options 'in excess of AV' on the ballot paper.

On the economy, Nick said that deficit reduction 'needs acceleration' and any agreement would need to express this. Nick added that they also wanted to see about £5 billion of extra spending in some areas from 2011, including schools, and they were prepared for taxes to rise to pay for this. Gordon said he was 'prepared to take tough decisions' on both spending and tax.

On Europe and defence there was little disagreement. The Lib Dems wanted Trident put into the strategic defence review but remained committed to the independent nuclear deterrent.

Then the discussion moved on to GB's position.

Gordon said the government needed to be 'thoroughly collegiate' and establish 'good ways of working closely'. 'I will not be a barrier to a change of personnel,' he added.

Nick started as soft cop. There was 'no animosity whatsoever' on his part to Gordon. 'But in our view it is not possible to secure the legitimacy of the coalition and win the referendum [on electoral reform] unless in a dignified way you move on.'

'You have been an incredible catalyst in reshaping politics,' he added emolliently. 'But I simply don't believe we can persuade the public that we are about renewal unless you go in time.'

What did Gordon think?

Gordon said his role was essential to form the government. He was also needed to ensure that the political reform programme got underway properly and to complete his work on 'securing the economic recovery'. As to timing, 'Once we have secured these objectives I will of course consider my position and be prepared to move on.'

That clearly wasn't the timetable that Clegg had in mind.

'Is it enough for you to stay on until the referendum?' he asked tentatively, on the assumption that the referendum would be before the end of the year.

'I am needed to get this coalition through the Labour Party,' Gordon responded, explaining that his commitment and persuasion would be needed to mobilise party support for the coalition and its programme, not only in the Cabinet but also the unions and the PLP.

Nick countered that it would be 'a massive political risk and gamble for the Lib Dems to legitimise a Prime Minister who was seen to have lost an election'.

'I will announce my intention,' said Gordon, suggesting that he would make a statement about his future when the coalition was announced. Reverting to the challenges ahead to get the coalition launched successfully, he said his approach to timing would be 'task driven'. There would also need to be a Labour leadership election, and that would take time.

At this point Danny came in as tough cop. For the coalition to succeed, he said bluntly, 'Gordon needs to go before the referendum.' He needed to be frank that in his view the referendum simply could not be won under Gordon's leadership.

Gordon responded as before. 'Look, someone has got to get Labour to do this.' Without him it would be hard if not impossible to get the coalition accepted by the various branches of the Labour Party and he was needed to handle the politics of the referendum.

Nick reverted to soft cop. 'We have all got to understand the fundamental psychological desire for change,' he said. 'As Peter said on Friday, we have got to "turn the page".' While there needed to be both stability and change, 'there has to be some sort of catharsis for people'. This could not come without a change of leadership.

Gordon came back to the referendum. The issue came down to 'whether it was easier or harder to win the referendum with or without me'. They needed to think this through further, and he would reflect on what had been said. And reflect not just on his position but also on the wider issue of the referendum. Should it be multi-option or just a single question on AV? Should it include a question on an elected Lords? Should there be a wider question on parliamentary reform, such as banning paid second jobs for MPs, which might help to make it genuinely popular?

Nick said he and his colleagues also needed to reflect further. It was agreed that he and Gordon would meet again at 10.30 the following morning, back in the House of Commons. Lib Dem MPs were meeting in the early afternoon, and his intention was to ask them to agree to start negotiations with Labour later in the day.

On that jagged note, the meeting ended.

•••

GB returned to No. 10 and immediately set to work on the policy note which Clegg had tabled. Reading it through, he was convinced that it was simply the note which the Lib Dems had tabled for their second round of talks with the Conservatives, but with a new heading: 'Liberal Democrat–Labour Party discussions, 9 May 2010'.

'Look, it's a list of things they have been discussing with the Tories,' he said to me, reading out items like 'in light of market concerns further and faster action on the deficit will be taken', 'an Emergency Budget will be presented within fifty days … [to] set out overall spending plans to eradicate the structural deficit over an expedited but responsible timescale', and 'a cut in the number of government ministers and in ministerial pay [will be made]'.

'It's the Tory agenda, without any progressive underpinning,' he said. 'What we need to do is to make them see that policy needs to follow from agreement on progressive principles and values. We can do that, the Tories can't. Without it, their coalition will be blown apart by events.'

Sitting at his PC in the now almost completely deserted war room, he started tapping out a letter to Clegg on progressive principles and values, which he intended to give him in the morning.

'Whatever we do needs to be founded on a big vision of social justice, liberty and a fair economic plan for Britain's future prosperity,' was his opening line. He also started amending the Lib Dem policy note to start in this way, rather than its narrow first sentence referring only to 'political and constitutional renewal' as the government's first objective.

On reading the three-page Lib Dem note, four things struck me.

First, on the economy, the pledge to eliminate the structural deficit over an 'expedited' timescale – which implied not just token acceleration of our already ambitious deficit reduction plans, but further very significant and early cuts – was there in black and white as a Lib Dem proposal, not a Tory proposal with which they were disagreeing. So if, as Gordon said, this is what they had been discussing with the Tories, then it looked as if it was also what they had agreed with them.

At the time, and in the negotiations on Monday and Tuesday, I thought they weren't serious about this, or did not understand what it would mean in practice. However, the centrepiece of George Osborne's Emergency Budget on 22 June was deficit reduction of £40 billion by 2014/15 over and above the £73 billion already set out by Alistair Darling, precisely to eliminate the structural deficit over an expedited timescale. 'Whose judgement, or ideology, do we trust – Keynes's or Osborne's?' wrote Keynes's biographer Robert Skidelsky after the Emergency Budget. For Nick Clegg and his negotiators, within just two days of the election, the answer was clearly 'Osborne's'. This was to make a policy agreement between the Lib Dems and the Tories possible. On this central strategic issue, they were at one.

Second, there was a comic mixing of the general with the specific. There was to be an Emergency Budget, expedited deficit reduction, a referendum on electoral reform, sweeping devolution of power and a fixed date for the next election of 'the first Thursday in May 2014' (at no stage in any of our discussions with the Lib Dems was a five-year fixed parliamentary term tabled by them or discussed between us; four years was always the term envisaged, and no 55 per cent parliamentary threshold for any early dissolution was ever mentioned). But alongside these appeared 'a commitment to reduce carbon emissions from the public sector by 10 per cent within twelve months', 'proposals for the roll-out of green mortgages' and 'implementation of an eco-cashback scheme'.

Third, the Lib Dem paper included a number of points where they couldn't conceivably have reached agreement with the Tories, unless these points had been added just for our benefit, which appeared unlikely given the drafting.

In this category was a commitment 'to bring forward a post-legislative referendum on alternative voting systems, to include the option of the Single Transferable Vote, no later than May 2011', 'a commitment to no public subsidy for nuclear power stations', 'a commitment not to raise the cap on tuition fees' and 'a new target of 40 per cent of energy to be from renewable sources by 2020'.

So it didn't look as if they were there yet with the Tories, however many individual policy concessions they may have secured. There was still something to play for.

•••

There was a fourth striking thing about the note. It was entirely silent on Europe. This was odd, I said to Gordon, if it was indeed the working text between the Lib Dems and the Tories. 'That's true. I'll press Clegg on that tomorrow,' Gordon said, looking at it again. 'How is he going to handle Europe with Cameron? They'll be plunged straight into battles over the Budget, the European recovery plan and the euro, and all the Tories will be saying is no, no, no.'

This omission was all the more notable because, as we speculated on the real political character behind the rhetorical façade, Nick Clegg's Europeanism increasingly seemed to me the essential thing that separated him from the Cameron Conservatives.

While I was on friendly terms with most of the leading

Lib Dems, I did not know Clegg well. He came to the fore
after I had left the Lib Dems for Labour in 1995. But what
I saw and heard reminded me to some extent of Tony Blair.
The easy public-school charm, looks and manners. The
instinctive anti-authoritarianism, with a ruthless streak. A
bit of a rebel, at an even posher public school (Westminster
plays Fettes) with wealthier parents, who liked to paint
himself as an Establishment outsider despite it all. Not
greatly interested in the Left–Right politics of distribution
and redistribution ('economics bores him and he doesn't
really have views on all this,' one of his advisers said when
we discussed tax-and-spend options). And another telling
Blair parallel: a student actor, not a student politician, at
Cambridge. Like Blair, he did not take to politics seriously until his mid-twenties, when he had to select a party,
operating from the political centre with light ideological
baggage.

That party might naturally have been the Tories.
Whereas Blair imbibed Christian socialism and became
a barrister pupil to Derry Irvine, Clegg's first, formative
political job was as adviser to a senior Tory. But it was in
Brussels; it was a pro-European Tory (Leon Brittan, then
trade commissioner); and his whole career and interests
were European to a degree which made a Tory career in the
1990s unsustainable. His objective was to become an MEP,
at a time when even Conservative Euro-pragmatists were
being hounded and deselected. The Dutch mother, Russian
aristocrat grandmother, Spanish wife, fluent European
languages, master's degree from the College of Europe in

Bruges, CV as a fast-rising Eurocrat – everything the Lib Dems loved and Tory associations would have distrusted if not loathed.

These were principled as well as pragmatic reasons for selecting the Lib Dems. But they were distinct from the radical Left liberalism which dominated the Liberal Party and later the Liberal Democrats from Jo Grimond in the 1960s to Paddy Ashdown and Charles Kennedy in the Blair decade, via David Steel and Roy Jenkins (who brought with him a large band of Labour social democrats). None of these leaders could conceivably have supported the David Laws introduction to *The Orange Book* of 2004, with its subtitle 'Reclaiming Liberalism' and its Gladstonian *cri de cœur*: 'How did it come about that over the decades up to the 1980s the Liberal belief in economic liberalism was progressively eroded by forms of soggy socialism and corporatism, which have too often been falsely perceived as a necessary corollary of social liberalism?' Words which pointed towards the economic Right and the possibility of accord with the Conservatives, and stony ground for the progressive Left instincts to which Gordon Brown was appealing.

•••

In any case, for Nick Clegg the issue wasn't only policy. It was Gordon Brown personally. If this wasn't clear enough from Peter's report of their late-night conversation in the Commons, it was soon to be.

It was 2.11 a.m. when Paddy left a voicemail message

on my Blackberry. 'Hi Andrew, it's Paddy here with David
Laws. We've got a bit of a crisis and I need to speak to you
urgently.' Deep asleep, I didn't hear the Blackberry's vibra-
tion. Nor did I hear it again at 5.37 a.m. when a text arrived
from Switch: 'Please come in at 06.30. Gordon.' But as I
read both messages at 6 a.m., the connection wasn't hard to
fathom. Nor the likely drama of the day ahead.

MONDAY 10 MAY

Monday 10 May was the day of Gordon Brown's first resignation – as Leader of the Labour Party. This was intended, and for some hours tentatively expected, to bring about a Lab–Lib coalition government. But it was not to be, and his second resignation, as Prime Minister, followed twenty-six hours later. This is how it happened.

•••

I returned Paddy's call at 6.30 a.m. He was on the phone and we only got to speak at 7.25 a.m. 'I only want to have one conversation like this,' he said in his endearingly peremptory Captain Ashdown manner. 'So could you discuss what I am going to say with Gordon, Peter and Alastair, and let's have just one conversation afterwards.'

The previous night's conversation between Gordon and Nick had been 'a disaster', Paddy said. Nick had gone in thinking that Gordon was going to give him a firm early date for his departure, and on that basis they could start negotiations for a Lib–Lab coalition, which was strongly supported by him (Paddy) and other key figures in the party. But instead Gordon had dug in and rowed back from the understanding Nick believed he had reached in their earlier Foreign Office conversation. Unless this changed, 'it will all be off, and you will have driven us into the arms of the Tories'.

I was cautious. A reliable intermediary had told me that Paddy had been asked by Nick to 'big up' the Labour alternative to the Tories, not least to give Nick a stronger hand to play with David Cameron. On the other hand, Gordon's future did have to be resolved before any serious Lab–Lib plan was going anywhere, and Gordon had said as much to me. It was a question of dates and context.

So I thought I'd better check I had got him right.

'Sorry, Paddy, can I be clear. You are saying that if there were an agreed early exit by GB, the only obstacle to a Labour coalition would be gone?'

'Yes.' Lib Dem MPs, he said, were meeting at 1 p.m. 'The question is whether Nick opens the way for a Lib–Lab coalition or continues on the Tory track. Gordon is the difference between the two.'

'Right. And Nick thought he was meeting GB to agree this last night?'

'Yes, in fact he thought they had agreed it in their earlier meeting. But instead Gordon dug in, said he needed to stay on for an indefinite period. Nick left in despair, and we have got one chance to put this back together again.'

Having had only a brief read-out by Peter of this part of the Gordon–Nick conversation (Gordon hadn't mentioned it to me at all; we had only talked policy and Clegg), I was flying blind.

'When would GB need to go to make this possible?' I asked.

'It needs to be soon. He needs a dignified exit, but it needs to be around the summer and announced at the outset.'

'So before the AV referendum, if we were to hold that in the late autumn?'

'Yes.'

'Well,' I said, calculating weeks and months in my mind. 'Being realistic, our party conference at the end of September sounds like the natural break point.'

We batted this around. The party conference was a dignified and orderly moment of transition. It gave time for a proper leadership election. It gave the time Gordon needed to embed the coalition within the Labour Party and pioneer the economic and political reform policies of the coalition. It also put a new leader in place before the start of the AV referendum campaign, assuming the referendum were held in November, which I was now clear was the earliest it could be held in any event.

Paddy thought this worked. There was the 'another unelected Prime Minister' point. But if that Prime Minister were David Miliband, then he didn't think this mattered particularly. 'Nor if it is his brother, though he's the second best,' Paddy added. David would be popular on all sides, would get on with Nick, and was manifestly qualified for the job. 'He's been a great Foreign Secretary, I really mean that.' Everything depended on winning the referendum and making a good start on the economy.

'But what about the Tories?' I asked. 'Aren't your Tory negotiations supposed to be going swimmingly?'

'Yes, they have made a good offer,' said Paddy. 'But not as good as Labour could make, particularly on the constitution. And we both know the wider progressive arguments. GB's the issue.'

'OK, let me see what's the score. This is a bit above my pay grade,' I said.

'It's very urgent,' was Paddy's passing shot, as if I wasn't aware.

•••

I immediately phoned David Laws. We had spoken the evening before, but before the second Clegg–Brown meeting. He was closer to the negotiations and, I thought, to Nick Clegg, and not so obviously Labour-leaning.

David was walking across Westminster Bridge, on his way in. I told him what Paddy had said. 'That's about right: Gordon is the major barrier,' he said. He also thought that Nick would have 'no problems at all' with David Miliband.

Walking to the tube to go to Downing Street, I texted Paddy about one issue which I didn't recall we had nailed down. 'Are we talking about a coalition agreement for a full four-year term?' I asked. 'Yep. I don't think anything else has been suggested,' he came back ten minutes later, by when I was squashed on the Victoria Line thinking how on earth the next steps were going to be handled.

I assumed that Peter would be up to speed and have a plan. Hopefully he was already speaking to Gordon. Danny

Alexander had texted me at 7 a.m. saying he couldn't raise Peter on his mobile and needed to speak to him before 8. I woke Peter on his home line, asking him to call Danny pronto. There was a text message from Peter as I got off the tube, asking that we meet in his Cabinet Office room at 9.30.

I was going to see Gordon imminently so I phoned Peter. He was on voicemail. So I called Alastair. He had also had Paddy on to him, and said Paddy had also phoned Tony Blair in the middle of the night, saying what he'd said to me.

As I paced up and down in front of the Ministry of Defence, not wanting to go into No. 10 without a plan, Alastair and I discussed the position. He had from the outset been more sceptical than me about dealing with the Lib Dems, but if Clegg was indeed determined not to support the Tories then the path ahead was clear. 'We can't hand the country over to the Tories if there is a viable alternative,' he said. He agreed that a leadership transition at party conference worked best for all concerned. 'OK, that's what we go for then,' I said, crossing Whitehall to go into No. 10 through 70 Whitehall.

•••

It was 8.30 a.m. Apart from a few officials, the only people in the war room were Gordon and Sarah, who was about to take the boys to school.

'I need to tell you what the Liberals have been telling me overnight,' I said to Gordon. We went into his inner office and shut the door.

I paraphrased what Paddy and David Laws had said to me, and our discussions, prefacing it with: 'Gordon, we have never really talked about how you see your own position going forward. But I know you want to forge a progressive government if it can be achieved, and this is what the Liberals are telling me.'

Gordon listened intently, then got up and paced around the room, responding calmly. He had clearly thought all this through.

'This can all be done,' he said. He said he had wanted to announce before the election, and then again in the final leaders' television debate a week before the poll, that he would only be staying until autumn 2011 in order to get clearly through the economic crisis and enact the next raft of major political reforms. 'I'm not clinging on once the job is done. The others were against my saying this, so we didn't, but that's my position.' What mattered to him above all else was keeping Labour in power.

So it came down to the difference between about five and eighteen months. I said it wasn't the number of months that counted but what was accomplished during them. By the party conference he could have achieved all his principal goals – the progressive coalition in place, economic recovery on the way, major constitutional reforms underway. And he would be handing the coalition over to another Labour Prime Minister.

It would only work, he said, if Clegg was genuinely asking him to stay until October. There was no question of him clinging on. And any announcement had to be made

by him before anything got out. He also needed to speak
to Sarah (who couldn't be contacted – she had gone from
dropping the boys at school to the hairdressers).

At this point Ed Balls came in, followed soon after by
Peter. They quickly agreed with the plan. The issue was
how to announce it and secure a coalition. We started talking about how and when announcements would be made,
when formal negotiations would start, when to call the
Cabinet, the Parliamentary Labour Party, the party's ruling
National Executive Committee and the so-called 'Clause 5'
joint meeting of the Cabinet and the NEC that would be
needed to ratify a coalition agreement. The letter to Clegg,
started the previous night, also had to be completed. Sue
Nye, David Muir and others joined, and logistics took shape
over the next hour before GB was due to see Clegg for the
third time.

After the immediate decisions, I left GB's office to phone
Paddy. As I came off the phone, a civil servant asked me the
state of play. 'Well, wait for it. It looks as if we may be about
to start negotiating a coalition with Clegg; and GB will
announce that as part of it he is standing down in October.'
Which is how it looked at 9.30 a.m.

•••

The 11.15 a.m. meeting with Nick Clegg (it got delayed from
10.30) was the last of the cloak-and-dagger affairs. Gordon
left by car from the back of No. 10, turning right into Horse
Guards Road, left onto the Mall and, via Buckingham

Palace and the backstreets between Victoria and Millbank, entering the Palace of Westminster by a back entrance. As his car sped out of Downing Street there was another media flurry. Had it turned right and onto the Mall because he was going to the Palace to resign? Even the helicopter lost him.

It was a businesslike meeting, as related by GB afterwards. Gordon explained what he was proposing to do in terms of leadership, if a coalition was for real. Nick said that Gordon's decision – about which he had been briefed – unlocked a potential coalition and said that on this basis he would recommend to his MPs in their 1 p.m. meeting that negotiations open with Labour on the same basis as had taken place with the Conservatives. He would continue dialogue with the Tories, but he hoped that a Lab–Lib coalition could now be secured, and the negotiations should start as soon as possible.

GB was precise about Clegg's intention to 'open negotiations with Labour on the same basis as with the Conservatives' when he debriefed us in No. 10 immediately afterwards. If carried through, this would have given strong momentum to Lab–Lib negotiations, which in turn, would have made far easier the task of rallying the PLP and the wider Labour Party, since the alternative was to oblige the Lib Dems to put David Cameron in power against their will, or face an immediate second election If they voted against a minority Tory government's Queen's Speech after Labour had refused to entertain a coalition. (It was to be sharply at variance with what in fact came out of the meeting of Lib Dem MPs at 4 p.m., when David Laws, on behalf of the party, said that that the Lib Dems were making 'very good progress' with the Tories and just needed 'clarification of details ... while we continue to listen to the representations that are coming from the leader of the Labour Party'. So in the intervening four hours Nick Clegg changed his mind or had it changed for him. But that is jumping ahead.)

Gordon also gave Nick the letter he had written about the imperative for progressive values to underpin a coalition, and they talked with animation – as GB recalled to me later – about the importance of fairness, internationalism and political modernisation as the foundations of a partnership. 'This is what I'm really interested in,' Nick said repeatedly. They also agreed that Gordon would make his leadership resignation statement immediately after Nick had announced the start of formal Lab–Lib negotiations, to give them maximum momentum. Nick said he would call Gordon once the Lib Dem parliamentary party meeting was over.

There was another telling exchange. Gordon was keen to get out a joint statement with the Lib Dems about the imperative for co-ordinated European action on growth as part of tackling the euro crisis.

GB said that he suggested to Nick that he get a draft over to Vince so he and Alistair could do this together. 'No, no, get it to my office, not to Vince,' he said Nick responded curtly.

'So that's why Vince is not part of their negotiating team,' said Peter. 'No love lost there.'

•••

Back in No. 10, ministers and senior MPs were briefed by phone on the likely start of negotiations, and drafting started on GB's leadership resignation statement. The Cabinet was summoned for 6 p.m. A meeting of the officers of the National Executive Committee was summoned for the Tuesday morning. These meetings were deliberately in advance of the meeting of the Parliamentary Labour Party on Wednesday. Gordon's intention was that the Cabinet and the NEC, which includes union and wider party representatives, should first endorse the Lab–Lib strategy; this, followed by decisive momentum in the negotiations themselves, would give maximum leverage for the meeting with all Labour MPs, where there was likely to be more dissent. The 'Clause 5' meeting was provisionally fixed for the Sunday, as the formal party mechanism to endorse the coalition.

All these steps were taken in a spirit of tentative expectation that we were moving towards a Lab–Lib coalition. An expectation because Gordon's decision to resign the leadership appeared to have cut the Gordian knot (a weak pun used on the day). It was the answer to senior internal party critics who said that GB simply couldn't continue in any event; and it was being done on a basis which the Lib Dems, including Nick Clegg personally, said made a Lib–Lab coalition possible or even likely.

Yet only a tentative expectation, because 'there's many a slip 'twixt cup and lip'. And despite the protestations of desire from the Lib Dems, including Clegg, their dialogue with the Conservatives had not cooled. On the contrary, the

Lib Dem team held a further ninety-minute meeting with the Tory team in 70 Whitehall while GB and Clegg were meeting in the Commons. As Danny Alexander left this session shortly before noon he told the cameras that the two teams had got on 'really well together' – identical words to William Hague's as he left moments before. At the very least, we and the Tories were being played off against each other. To what end wasn't, we sensed, decided even by Clegg and his immediate colleagues, although the tension between the Ashdown and Cable 'progressives' who gravitated naturally towards Labour, and David Laws's 'Orange Book liberals', who had no difficulty endorsing Tory ambitions for 'further and faster cuts', was fairly evident. A text I sent to Paddy shortly after seeing Danny's positive statement about the Tory talks summed up our unease: 'All on course. Big issue resolved. Essential Nick is generous in public about GB. Asked him to lead government until Oct etc.'

Paddy called back to say that all was on course. But it wasn't. We waited anxiously for the Lib Dem parliamentary party meeting to end so that Gordon could make his statement and negotiations could start. Three o'clock came and went, then 3.30 and 3.45. Suddenly BBC News 24 went over to a crackly David Laws making a statement outside the Commons committee room where the Lib Dem meeting was breaking up. The BBC broadcast him live via a journalist's mobile phone. He was saying that they had had 'very good negotiations with the Tories' and would now be seeking 'further clarification of details' of aspects of the Tory offer – 'details, details', Peter and I said in unison to the giant screen in the war room, while David Laws was adding: 'The parliamentary party has agreed that the leader will continue to listen to the representations that are coming from the leader of the Labour Party.'

'So it's negotiating final details with the Tories while listening to see if we've got anything to say,' Alastair said.

'Not what we were told at all; they are playing games,' said Peter emphatically.

'Or perhaps this is Nick's idea of moving towards us in stages,' I said more optimistically.

The imperative now was for Gordon to speak to Clegg to understand what was going on, and then to make his leadership resignation statement before it leaked.

A few minutes later, Clegg came on the line.

It had been a long meeting with lots of views expressed, he began. 'But to get to the point, lots of people want to open talks with you,' he said. However, there were 'huge risks of the smaller party being the minnow swallowed up by two whales', and they needed 'some form of down payment' about a change in the electoral system because this mattered so much to his colleagues.

'What kind of down payment?' Gordon asked.

'We are relaxed about the terms and conditions of a coalition,' he said, 'provided legislation on AV can be brought forward subject to final agreement in a referendum.' A strong view had been expressed that the AV legislation should take effect even before a referendum, 'but I think I agree with you that it requires a referendum before coming in,' he said, referring to their earlier conversation.

'It's essential that we can't be massacred,' Nick went on, explaining why AV was so important to him. He said David Cameron hadn't responded on AV since he (Clegg) had raised the issue, beyond noting that the Conservatives had voted against it in the past, although he was 'clearly desperate to do a deal'.

Gordon confirmed that Labour would definitely offer AV legislation and a referendum. The issue now was the status of the Lib–Lab talks and what they both said in their forthcoming statements. People needed to understand that the talks were for real.

They were for real, Clegg responded. 'Lots of people would just walk if we went in with the Tories.'

But, GB pressed, would he say that the talks with Labour were on the same basis as with the Tories?

'Well, we don't want to bounce ourselves,' said Clegg, uneasily. He suggested that after GB's statement he say something like: 'You and I have talked. We intend to continue our existing dialogue with the Tories and we now also wish take forward discussions with the Labour Party.'

But, GB asked again, would this mean formal negotiations with Labour on the same basis as with the Tories? In his own statement, he said, he was proposing to talk about negotiations for 'a progressive government' with progressive economic plans for jobs, growth and deficit reduction, able to meet the demand for electoral reform.

'I don't want to do this in a muddle,' said Clegg, now still more uneasy. 'I don't want to screw things up. I want to talk to a couple of people and call back in five minutes, if that's OK.'

So the Laws mobile phone statement was indeed the Lib Dems' considered position. They wanted to negotiate a final deal with the Tories while merely listening to representations from Labour. This wasn't going to work, we all said as the call ended, and started discussing what this meant for GB's imminent statement.

A few minutes later, Clegg came through again to say that they would state in terms that they wished to open 'negotiations' with Labour. This was a step forward, but it still left the question as to what Clegg himself would say about GB's departure. Here again, Nick proposed some bland words, and started reading wording about GB's announcement being a positive statement in the national interest. Those of us listening in shook our heads again. This was getting uncomfortable for Gordon personally.

Peter, who was listening to the call in the war room, walked into the inner office where GB was speaking and waved to Gordon to put him on. 'I think Peter may be able to help here,' GB said. 'Good, put him on,' said Nick eagerly, 'we need to get this right.'

'Nick, I don't think what you are proposing to say is clear enough if we all want this to succeed,' said Peter. 'It needs to be much clearer: you need to find the right way of saying that should your talks with the Labour Party be successful, it would be important for Gordon to continue to play his role in the months ahead. For this coalition government to work, and for us to make the changes that we face in the country, we would need this man's experience and skills, which is why I want him to continue for the coming months.'

Nick, clearly taking notes, said 'OK, OK' and that he would speak 'in this kind of way in my own words', and the call ended.

Once again, Nick wanted Lab–Lib discussions, but supported by weak and uncertain statements as to their status and where they might lead. However, we had no time to debate this further. GB's statement had to be made as soon as possible. He wanted to go out into Downing Street and make it to the media camp there and then, but Iain Bundred persuaded him to give a little notice so that the main political reporters could be present. It was set for 5 p.m., and delivered from the lectern in front of the No. 10 door.

•••

Gordon's Monday statement stunned the political world, much as had David Cameron's initial statement offering the Lib Dems a coalition on Friday afternoon. It opened up a serious Lab–Lib coalition alternative to the Tory–Lib Dem arrangement which by then had been nearly four days in the making.

There was no prevarication in Gordon's statement either about the credibility of a progressive coalition or about his intention to resign the leadership to make that possible:

> If it becomes clear that the national interest, which is stable and principled government, can be best served by forming a coalition between the Labour Party and the Liberal Democrats, then I believe I should discharge that duty to

form that government which would in my view command a majority in the House of Commons in the Queen's Speech and any other confidence votes.

But I have no desire to stay in my position longer than is needed to ensure the path to economic growth is assured and the process of political reform we have agreed moves forward quickly. The reason that we have a hung parliament is that no single party and no single leader was able to win the full support of the country. As leader of my party, I must accept that that is a judgement on me. I therefore intend to ask the Labour Party to set in train the processes needed for its own leadership election. I would hope that it would be completed in time for the new leader to be in post by the time of the Labour Party conference. I will play no part in that contest and I will back no individual candidate.

Gordon walked back into the packed war room to spontaneous applause from assembled staff and ministers, who had been watching it gathered around the giant TV screens. Peter and several aides were in tears. 'Thanks, but back to work, back to work,' Gordon said with a broad smile, motioning everyone to sit.

'That's done the business. Now we need everyone out there,' he said, looking at Alastair, Douglas and me, standing together by the Sky screen. The three of us left for College Green in Douglas's car to do a live media round.

On College Green, the media debated a scene transformed. 'Game-changer' was the word of the hour. The question was, how would the – currently silent – Tories react? Would the Lab–Lib negotiations make as rapid progress as the Tory–Lib negotiations?

Nick Clegg's reaction, when it finally came on Sky TV more than an hour later, was lawyerly and weaker than Peter's formulation. But it did the job of pointing to a possible Lab–Lib coalition in the wake of Gordon's resignation:

> Gordon Brown has made an important announcement today. It must have been a very difficult thing for him to say personally but I think he has taken it in the national interest and I think his announcement could be an important element in the smooth transition towards a stable government that people deserve, without of course prejudice and without predicting what the outcome of the talks will be between ourselves and the Labour Party.

Pundits started chewing over the intense Brown–Cameron competition now taking place for Clegg's support. They also relished an on-air shouting match between Alastair Campbell and Sky's Adam Boulton, an immediate YouTube hit.

•••

The Cabinet at 6 p.m., less than an hour after Gordon's leadership resignation statement, was to be the last formal ministerial meeting of thirteen years of New Labour rule. But it could hardly have been less elegiac. It was the most electric and urgent Cabinet of my year as a member. It was far from clear that it would be either Gordon's or Labour's last Cabinet, and Gordon certainly wasn't treating it as such.

The official Cabinet, with civil servants present, spent the first quarter of an hour on the euro crisis and Afghanistan. Sir Gus O'Donnell and his colleagues then withdrew, and ninety minutes of intense discussion of Lab–Lib coalition prospects took place in a 'political Cabinet', hurried at the end by the need for the negotiators to get to the first formal session with the Lib Dems set for 7.30 p.m., for which we were by then already late.

Gordon started with his by now well-rehearsed arguments. 'The numbers' were there for a Lab–Lib coalition without deals with the minor parties. The imperative was for a principled progressive coalition to secure the economic recovery and carry political reform. The policy basis for such a coalition was unproblematic. Summarising his discussions with Nick Clegg, he asked the Cabinet to agree that negotiations now start. He emphasised trade union support for such a coalition: 'They are absolutely clear that we should govern with the Liberals rather than let them put the Tories in, with all that would mean for the public services and union members.' The Cabinet, the PLP and the NEC on behalf of the wider party would be kept informed of progress and asked to ratify any coalition programme. 'Now that I have resigned the leadership, I have no personal advantage in this at all,' he emphasised. 'This isn't about me; it's about Labour, and whether we can give the country the change it wants, and I believe we can.'

Gordon asked me to summarise the policy issues at stake. To be properly heard I had to move from my usual seat at the end of the oval table to the vacant Cabinet Secretary's seat next to Gordon, because five members of the Cabinet were participating by conference call via a spider phone in front of him. 'It's like a séance,' Gordon quipped as the spider phone was passed along to move it closer to a later speaker. 'No, we aren't in the afterlife yet,' someone quipped.

I was relentlessly upbeat about coalition prospects with the Lib Dems, saying there were no obvious show-stoppers and on the face of it we were far closer to the Lib Dems on policy than were the Tories on the two key areas of electoral reform and the economy. (I deliberately didn't refer to the fact that the Lib Dems appeared comfortable with the Tory position on significantly 'further and faster' deficit reduction, assuming they would not insist on this in negotiations with us.) Labour in particular could offer a referendum on AV, for which we would campaign in support, which the Tories couldn't. But the devil would be in a lot of detail and we would all need to engage on this.

Peter Mandelson and Harriet Harman spoke next, followed by a *tour de table* punctuated by ethereal contributions from the spider phone.

Most of the mini-speeches – which is the nature of Cabinet discussion in a body of nearly thirty members – were in strong or measured support of a Lab–Lib coalition, starting with Peter and Harriet. Harriet, in clear, straightforward support of GB, said, 'We shouldn't lose sight of the fact that it was a remarkable election result, coming after three terms in office, the economic crisis, the expenses crisis, and the feral media and the Tory millions.' Gordon was 'putting the interests of the country and the party first' in pursuing Lib Dem coalition while announcing his intention to stand down soon. The arguments for a coalition came down to one simple fact. 'I fear the Tories and their impact on the people I represent. I couldn't go back to my constituency and say that we could have put in place an alternative government to the Tories, but we didn't because we didn't particularly like the Lib Dems.'

This 'principled duty to stop the Tories and forge a progressive alliance if we can' argument was broadly supported by the great majority of the Cabinet, including Alan Johnson, David Miliband, Ed Miliband, Ed Balls, Hilary Benn, Peter Hain, Ben Bradshaw, Jim Murphy, Shaun Woodward, Yvette Cooper, John Denham, Jim Knight, Jan Royall, Bob Ainsworth, Tessa Jowell and Douglas Alexander. 'There's going to be either a Labour or a Tory Prime Minister coming out of this,' said Ed Miliband, 'and for the people we serve, it needs to be a Labour one.' David Miliband said there were 'grave risks – no one won, but we lost'. Nevertheless, 'Cameron has legitimised coalition government by offering one to the Lib Dems rather than just saying 'I've won, you've lost', and in those circumstances we are absolutely entitled to seek to govern in coalition.' The tests were how to keep the government in power into the medium term and how to carry big reforms with no automatic majority. John Denham was blunt: 'We need to present this as the best attainable government. If we don't seize it the Tories could lock us out of power for a generation.' So was Ben Bradshaw: 'Don't just hand power to the Tories. We have as good a right to govern in coalition with the Lib Dems as had Brandt and Schmidt when, as the second largest party, they governed with the FDP – and we regard them as great historic progressive German governments.' Jim Knight was briefest: 'Go for it.'

Peter Mandelson took a more nuanced line. A Lab–Lib Dem coalition was the right course 'but the Lib Dems will need to stop being normal opportunist Lib Dems', he said. 'We will have to be the ones holding them to a responsible course, particularly in view of the incredibly lavish, sky's-the-limit, absolutely desperate strategy of the Tories to getting the Lib Dems into an alliance.' This hit an anti-Lib Dem vein, but in the cause of coalition if it could be secured on reasonable terms. The evident sceptics, notably Alistair Darling and Jack Straw, adopted this position, declaring themselves not opposed to the principle of talks but raising the spectre of real problems in working with the Lib Dems in practice and settling the details of a coalition agreement. 'We have been fighting the Lib Dems like cats and dogs', said Jack, 'even if our programmes aren't that different. And I remember 1974 and all those knife-edge votes.' Alistair said: 'I have no difficulty in speaking to Liberals. There is a lot of common ground, but how much detail would we need to agree on and can we agree, particularly on the economy?'

Liam Byrne and Sadiq Khan took a nuanced dissenting line. 'Many of the PLP think it better to renew in opposition,' said Liam, 'and they positively relish the idea of the Liberals doing a deal with the Tories.' But only Andy

Burnham struck a clear note of opposition. 'While we might be able to stitch something together, it won't be renewal and the country won't listen to us,' he said. 'The public will find it a surprise; it will build up resentment and we will find ourselves punished in an election in twelve to eighteen months' time.'

The position of the minor parties was raised several times, but not as a particular problem. Shaun Woodward said that all the Northern Ireland parties would either actively support Labour or abstain, without any sectarian deals. 'The DUP hate the Tories; Cameron has been trying to wipe them out.' Peter Hain said Labour's coalition in Wales with Plaid Cymru 'had fierce critics inside the party when it was formed in 2007, but it has been a success and they will support us in Westminster'. Jim Murphy said it was 'essential we don't negotiate with the SNP, although they are desperate to negotiate with us'. 'Alex Salmond keeps leaving beseeching messages for me to call him,' interjected Peter. 'Don't become a suitor under any circumstances,' said Jim to laughter. 'The SNP could not vote against us on any confidence vote without being massacred in next year's Scottish elections.'

Gordon summed up that the Cabinet was agreed that negotiations should now start. He also wanted departmental heads to talk to their opposite Lib Dem numbers during the evening. As to the negotiating team, it would be Harriet, Peter and myself – then, he added, a bit hesitantly, 'because I know there are others who have views' – 'Ed Miliband and Ed Balls'. This provoked an outburst from Bob Ainsworth on the spider phone that he wasn't happy with that team, but GB cut him short, saying he would speak to him afterwards. 'I promise each of you a report back and a further Cabinet before any decisions are finalised,' he said.

As he was speaking, a note was passed to me. 'Hague has just said the Tories will give Clegg a referendum on AV!!' I showed this to Gordon as the Cabinet was breaking up. 'We've got to go as fast as possible on AV,' GB said. He repeated this as parting advice to the negotiating team as we gathered in No. 11 before leaving for Portcullis House. 'There's got be a referendum, but do the legislation in parallel, or something like that, so it can be brought in immediately after the referendum. We can't have the Lib Dems claiming they have got nothing to choose between us and the Tories on this.'

•••

Whereupon we decamped in cars to Portcullis House, which in contrast to just two days previously – although it seemed more like two weeks – was heaving with MPs, staff and journalists, all throwing questions, comments and knowing glances as we passed on the way to the lifts to the same third-floor conference room overlooking Big Ben where we met on the Saturday.

This time the Lib Dems were there ahead of us. Sir Gus O'Donnell was also present, and began proceedings with words of welcome and best wishes, adding that as with the talks between the Lib Dems and the Tories, he and his colleagues stood ready to assist as needed. He then left, and the civil service played no further part in the negotiations. The Lib Dems did not want any officials present at any stage 'because they will just be the arm of government and this is a political exercise', Danny Alexander insisted.

Over the next eighty minutes until shortly after 9.30 p.m., when the Lib Dems had to leave for another session of their MPs, two different meetings took place in Room 319 of Portcullis House. There was the meeting that took place in the room itself. And there was the meeting which was briefed by the Lib Dem team to their MPs and the media afterwards.

The meeting proper started with pleasantries from Danny, who said he knew it 'had been a difficult and emotional time for you with Gordon's announcement'. Peter said that for our part the intention was to seek to form a coalition which would be a 'fresh, completely new government, based on real compromises between us, and not just a continuation of the existing Labour government with some Lib Dem participation'. This statement was welcomed by Danny, who tabled a revised version of the Lib Dem policy note which Nick Clegg had given GB the previous evening. This largely replicated the previous note but with two new commitments: that there should be immediate legislation to enact the AV electoral system, separate from a referendum on electoral reform, and also immediate legislation to create 'a fully elected second chamber'.

Danny suggested we start by discussing the economic proposals in the note. David Laws reiterated that the Lib

Dems wanted to see 'further and faster' deficit reduction than Labour's existing plan to halve the deficit within the next four years. As part of this, they now favoured immediate in-year cuts, with half the saving going into deficit reduction and half into new stimulus measures. David repeated Chris Huhne's argument in Saturday's meeting that the fall in the value of sterling made immediate cuts possible without an impact on the recovery. They also wanted to see a significant immediate start made on their £17 billion plan to raise the income tax threshold to £10,000, and a bank levy. To set all this out they favoured an Emergency Budget within a few weeks. They had also seen a Treasury note on immediate cuts, which the Conservatives had commissioned, which satisfied them that £6 billion of immediate cuts could be carried through without damaging the recovery.

Ed Balls responded that we agreed there should be a new economic statement for the new government after the Queen's Speech, including progress towards a higher tax threshold within a credible funding envelope. But not an Emergency Budget. And was it economically or politically sensible to go faster than Labour's existing ambitious plans to halve the deficit within four years starting in 2011, which the Lib Dems had so recently supported in the election? He probed on what was meant by the proposed commitment to 'expedite' elimination of the 'structural deficit', which implied big extra cuts? David did not offer figures, but said this was essential for 'credibility with the markets'. Ed disagreed.

It was left that both sides would reflect on all this further overnight. Peter said it would be a good idea if Vince Cable and Alistair Darling could engage directly on the tax/spending issues, and on the Lib Dems' bank levy plans, before we discussed them again. Danny didn't object but said, 'Agreements have to be made here.'

The discussion then turned to constitutional reform. Andrew Stunell pressed again on the Wright Committee and its proposal to give an elected committee control of timetabling government business in the Commons. He objected 'very strongly' to Peter's statement on Saturday that this could be 'a rod for our backs'. 'If this coalition is going to be about the new politics, then you have got to stop wanting to control everything,' he said bluntly. Harriet, who as Leader of the Commons had been in the thick of the Wright Committee discussions, said there wasn't a problem here. It was just a question of phasing the implementation of Wright's recommendations, and ensuring they proved workable in relation to other areas of Commons business before they were extended to the crucial area of government business. This appeared to take the trick.

The discussion then turned to fixed-term parliaments and electoral reform. We agreed quickly on four-year fixed-term parliaments and the need for a 'constructive vote of no confidence' arrangement, similar to Germany's, for early elections when a government fell. Would we whip on the AV legislation? Yes. Even before a referendum? Yes, as long as the legislation provided for a referendum before it took effect. Were we sure our troops would follow on this? Yes, on AV, but we couldn't go beyond AV although we were open to the Lib Dems also having a proportional representation option on the ballot paper if they wished.

The Lib Dems also wished the AV legislation to take effect immediately, including for by-elections, even before a referendum. I said this was impossible to justify. Chris Huhne said it would be on an 'experimental basis'. 'What, including an experimental general election?' I enquired. He said they expected the referendum to have been held by then.

I noted that the latest Lib Dem note included immediate legislation for an elected Lords. Did this really mean a first-session Bill? The first parliamentary session would already be preoccupied with difficult legislation for the Alternative Vote, a referendum on AV, and fixed-term parliaments. The Lords Reform Bill would be huge and very controversial in the Lords. Wouldn't it be better to agree the Lords plan in the first session and then legislate in the second session? Chris Huhne disagreed. 'The AV Bills are fairly short and straightforward and there will be plenty of time for Lords reform and other measures now we won't have your usual bevy of Home Office Bills.'

'Are you sure about that, Chris?' I said. 'I don't want to be the voice of the old politics, but I can't see us getting all this through in a first session, with the Lords fighting tooth and nail against its extinction, as it will.' This provoked Andrew Stunell into further remarks about the new politics, and how the Lib Dems would not be fobbed off by assurances that delayed key reforms 'for which we have been waiting for a century or more'. I observed that if we got everything else through in the first session, with a clear legislative plan for the Lords in place for the second session, that would be as bold as anything Mr Gladstone ever managed. Again, we agreed to consider further overnight.

Next came the Lib Dems' proposed 'Freedom Bill'. Here we were prepared to give a lot of ground. I said we were prepared to suspend or cancel the main ID card scheme and move in the Lib Dems' direction on the DNA database. What about ID cards for foreign nationals, who were already required to have documentation? These were totally unnecessary, said Chris. On the DNA database, again, should we dispose of all existing DNA data on those acquitted of serious crimes after three years, without even waiting for a review of the operation of the Scottish system? Yes, said Chris. I said we needed to consult further with Alan Johnson overnight. I thought we had a deal here.

Time was now running out. There was a brief discussion, led by Ed Miliband, of nuclear power, and what the Lib Dems meant by eliminating all public subsidies, and the credibility of a 40 per cent target for renewable energy by 2020, which Ed said no one in the energy world thought remotely attainable. The Lib Dems raised the Heathrow third runway. Would we agree to its cancellation? Peter started to respond that this was difficult because of its business impact. I intervened to say that we were considering this issue but, again, needed to reflect overnight. (I hadn't had a chance to tell Peter that I had already agreed with Gordon that we should delay the third runway and set up an independent review to consider airport expansion in the south-east.)

There was a concluding discussion on university tuition

fees. Peter noted from their paper that the Lib Dems weren't calling for abolition of the existing fees, which was a big shift. But what about the ongoing Browne review of student finance? Could we as a coalition agree to consider its report, without prejudice to Lib Dem opposition to fees? If we didn't, 'I really don't know where the money is going to come from to prevent a reduction in student places.' Danny said he didn't see how they could move further on this.

Danny asked if what we agreed would bind our new leader. 'Yes,' Peter replied.

Peter and Danny both ended by saying that the discussion had been constructive and we would both consider further the points raised before meeting at ten in the morning. Both sides would produce notes of outstanding issues for that meeting.

The Lib Dems left first, further handshakes all round, to go to their parliamentary party meeting. Staying for a few minutes to discuss the outcome, we all thought it had been good progress for a first formal eighty-minute meeting, a fraction of the time the Lib Dems had already spent with the Tories. Peter's concern was that Alistair and Vince needed to get to grips bilaterally with an economic package. He said he would arrange this and reported later that a meeting had been fixed for eleven in the morning, in parallel with the next meeting of the two negotiating teams. We could make further progress on this after they had met.

•••

It was 9.45 p.m. Harriet left for *Newsnight*, the two Eds went home, while Peter and I crossed Whitehall to No. 10 to brief GB and No. 10 officials and to commission overnight policy work.

As we broke up, someone mentioned to no particular surprise or comment that John Reid had been on TV attacking a Lab–Lib deal. More critics were bound to come out, and getting a broadly united PLP on side was a challenge to come. But the way forward seemed reasonably straightforward and attainable: to accelerate momentum in the negotiations on Tuesday so that a credible coalition proposal could be put to the Cabinet and the NEC for them to endorse in the immediate run-up to the meeting of the Labour MPs now fixed for Wednesday afternoon. The strong Cabinet endorsement of the coalition strategy, on the back of Gordon's resignation, was the critical factor.

It may or may not have worked. There were plenty of Labour MPs only too eager for opposition. But we were never to know. For a rather different meeting of the Lab–Lib negotiators was soon to be presented to Lib Dem MPs, which had the effect of ending Lab–Libbery for good.

•••

After half an hour in the war room discussing overnight work for the negotiations, I caught the start of *Newsnight* on the giant screen before walking up to the Prime Minister's flat at the top of No. 11 to brief Gordon. 'Do you think you have done enough tonight to get the Liberal Democrats to sign up?' was Kirsty Wark's opening question to a straight-bat Harriet. It still sounded very much game-on. Apart from John Reid, all the senior Labour reaction had so far been positive.

Gordon was having a glass of wine with Alistair Darling around the table of his cramped kitchen, discussing how Alistair would handle his economic discussion with Vince Cable in the morning.

'Look, this is all about politics, not policy,' Gordon was saying of the Lib Dem plan to raise the income tax threshold. 'Obviously we'll have to pay for it elsewhere, but we've got to be political like the Tories on this. They are giving the Liberals carte blanche.'

'I'll play my part,' said Alistair, 'but I can't have even bigger IOUs floating around the Treasury.'

'There won't be. It's politics, not policy…' said GB again.

'I know, but some of us will still have to deal with all this after you have ridden off into the sunset,' said Alistair in good-natured but weary banter, having been up most of the previous night at the EU finance ministers' crisis meeting on the euro.

Alistair left a few minutes later, and I took stock with Gordon over another glass of wine. It would come down to Alistair and Vince hammering out a deal on the Lib Dem tax-and-spending plans, and the Lib Dems being convinced we could and would deliver, soon, on AV, we agreed. He said he had been speaking to Ming Campbell and Vince, and they both favoured a Labour deal. Gordon was sure the party remained manageable. There was an NEC meeting in the morning, which would endorse the negotiations. The only hostile ministerial reaction he had had since Cabinet was from Bob Ainsworth – about the negotiators, not the principle of negotiations.

•••

As I left No. 10 at 11.15 p.m. to head to the tube and home, another dramatic text arrived from Paddy:

> This is not going well. The meeting with you guys was a disaster. The Tories will give us MASSIVELY more than you guys and were respectful where your body language was my guys said truly shocking. We need to speak urgently. This will not finish before midnight. Will you be up then? P.

He was texting from the Lib Dem parliamentary party meeting. I said I'd call when I got home.

I didn't understand Paddy's message at all. In no way had the meeting been a disaster; it hadn't even gone badly. As for body language, there had been frank discussion, but no disrespect or rudeness. Ed Balls had been typically vigorous on the case against immediate cuts and faster deficit reduction, but no more than Chris Huhne and Andrew Stunell on their constitutional reform and Home Office wish list. Anyway, we had only met for eighty minutes, a fraction of the time the Lib Dems had by now spent with the Tories. They couldn't have expected us to have reached agreement across the piece. But my view was that we had made good progress, particularly on constitutional reform, where we were offering what the Tories could not offer: support for AV in a referendum.

It sounded to me like gamesmanship – 'the talks are going badly, the Tories are offering the earth, and you need to raise your offer to stay in the game'. I also wondered whether an alibi was in the process of construction – 'the talks with Labour show they aren't serious about a coalition of equals, so we've got no choice but to go in with the Tories who are so much more constructive and respectful'.

By the time I got home, queries from journalists were also arriving about 'negative body language' on the part of Ed Balls and Ed Miliband. The 'talks having gone badly' was clearly being briefed by the Lib Dems just as the 'terrible' conversation between Clegg and Brown was briefed on the Saturday. The claims about 'negative body language' I thought particularly telling. Going for body language, rather than the substance of the negotiation, was something impossible to refute, particularly when everyone knows that Ed Balls gives as good as he gets in any discussion, though no more than Andrew Stunell or Chris Huhne.

Peter and I spoke on these lines – he was also getting calls – before I returned Paddy's call after half-past midnight.

Paddy was typically blunt. The Lib Dem negotiators had spoken one after another at the meeting; 'it was like a "Come to Jesus" moment', someone else said to me. They were unanimous that we weren't offering enough and were a league behind the Tories in all respects. What hadn't we been prepared to agree? I asked. The things he rattled off (third runway, ID cards, DNA, House of Lords, pupil premium) were either things we had in fact agreed, or had said we would consider further. I noted that he didn't mention further and faster deficit reduction, which was in fact the key area of disagreement. On 'body language', he said the word was that Peter and I had been friendly and constructive, Ed Balls and Ed Miliband the opposite. 'You need to get your team in line pdq, with a better offer, or this is going nowhere tomorrow.'

I disputed the body language. On policy, I said that this was all work in progress and we hadn't had much time to get going compared to the time already spent with the Tories. I started to go through the issues, but he didn't want to discuss 'these details'.

'Are you sure your guys really want to do a deal and aren't simply softening you up for the Tories?' I asked.

'We'll do a deal if you offer a good one. Nick is still absolutely even-minded on this, so you've got to get your act together,' he said.

After a last mini-lecture on why we needed to stop thinking like a government and start thinking like a supplicant for power, we ended.

•••

It was past 1 a.m. One day which had changed the face of British politics was ending. Another was about to start.

TUESDAY 11 MAY

'I don't like what is taking place at all…'

David Blunkett was speaking with fluent urgency on Radio 4's *Today* programme as I walked into the war room just after 7.30 a.m. 'What doesn't he like?' I asked rhetorically. 'GB, Clegg, you…' said a civil servant.

A few of us gathered round to listen.

'… I don't believe it will bring stability and I feel that the British people will feel that we have not heard what they said to us…'

This was a repeat of John Reid on the BBC the night before, but more damaging, from the heart of the PLP at the start of make-or-break day.

'… anyway, can you trust the Liberal Democrats? They are behaving like every harlot in history. What do the British people feel as they watch? Not what a small group of people in each of the major parties negotiating feel in what is increasingly looking a bunker, but what do people out in the country feel…'

In the bunker, it was a grim feeling of the Labour Party fragmenting. 'Are there others saying this publicly?' I asked one of the political staff. 'Only seven or eight backbenchers so far, but the day is yet young,' he replied.

'… it would be a coalition of the defeated, cobbled together, uncertain whether it can carry anything night by night, people dying – as they did when I first came into Parliament – on average about once every three months because of the nature of the sittings, and then a general election on the back of that. You don't have to be involved in politics to see what it would do to the Labour Party and its vote…'

'Have we got anyone going up?' I asked, as David was delving back into the dog days of 1974, his first election –

'… what would the nation have felt, if Jeremy Thorpe had cobbled together a coalition with Ted Heath, and the will of the nation to get rid of the Heath government and settle with the miners had been thwarted…'

'Only Tessa Jowell,' was the reply.

John Reid, meanwhile, was even more fiercely on the attack on *GMTV*. A Lab–Lib pact would be 'mutually assured destruction for both parties'. He, David and, we presumed, others, had been speaking overnight.

The possibility of a Lab–Lib coalition was slipping away, unless we could achieve significant momentum in the morning session of the negotiations.

•••

GB came down from the flat a few minutes later. We started going through the policy paper to be tabled at the 10 a.m. meeting of the negotiators.

'It all comes down to the economy now,' said GB. 'Alistair and Vince need to agree an economic package.'

No one had much of a handle on this. No. 10 and Treasury advisers hadn't made much progress overnight. GB called Alistair and asked him to join us. While we waited, Peter and the two Eds arrived.

From one source or another they had all heard about the previous night's talks having gone 'badly' and the two Eds' body language being 'appalling'. All gamesmanship, we agreed; but the Eds promised GB with mock seriousness that they would be on their best behaviour at 10 a.m. and not allow so much as a grimace to cross their faces.

We also discussed overnight conversations with MPs and ministers, and how to handle the party's National Executive meeting, fixed in parallel with the 10 a.m. meeting. GB planned to hit the phones himself.

I slipped out to catch Paddy Ashdown on the *Today* programme. Paddy was strongly positive about a Labour coalition, which was something. But then there was George Osborne, who dismissed the idea of a Tory minority government with great confidence in favour of an arrangement with the Lib Dems. 'We can't just turn up at Buckingham Palace and say we'd like to form a minority government; we would need the consent of the Liberal Democrats to form a minority government.'

Significant, I thought: ruling out going it alone. And the Tories who hadn't spoken. While we were splintering, the Tories were the model of public unity. Not a single Tory right-winger had been on the attack. Their side was desperate for power; too many on ours were desperate to give it up.

•••

GB and Alistair spoke much as the night before. Gordon had no doubt a deal could be done. Alistair didn't want new commitments pushing up the deficit. If Vince was going to pay for his £10,000 tax threshold and other pledges with cuts and tax rises elsewhere, 'he needs to be clear what he has got in mind or we will be up the proverbial without a paddle'.

'But of course I'll do what's possible,' he said. 'Anyway, Vince is definitely coming. He's asked for a Treasury car to fetch him. Getting used to ministerial life.'

Paddy was on the phone. Why were there no Labour voices on the media supporting a deal? 'It's just Blunkett, Reid and a string of your antis.'

GB said we had to get supportive ministers 'out there'. But we didn't want to put up any of the negotiators, who were anyway soon to leave for Portcullis House. It was a few crucial hours before Alan Johnson, Ben Bradshaw and others did supportive media rounds.

•••

Peter, Harriet, the two Eds and I left No. 10 at 9.50 a.m. for the third and final meeting with the Lib Dems in Room 319 of Portcullis House. Ed Miliband stopped at the café in the large atrium on the ground floor of Portcullis House to buy coffee and pastries to take up for everyone, 'so they can see I'm really, really committed to this going well', he said with a broad grin.

At two hours twenty minutes, this was by far the longest of the three Lab–Lib Dem meetings, although far shorter than the key Lib Dem–Tory meetings, including the one which was to follow our meeting in the afternoon. In all, the Lib Dems spent four and a half hours with us, but more than three times as long with the Conservatives. We never even got to the composition of a joint working text of an agreement, let alone negotiations on detailed wording.

This time it was not a case of two meetings – one in the room and another retold afterwards. There was only one meeting. In the room and retold, it was equally scratchy, and there was little momentum towards coalition. We kept getting stuck on second-order issues. Personalities grated. Blackberrys and mobiles came into action on both sides, with messages passing not only in and out of the room, including commentary on the state of play, but also within the room as Danny and Peter sought to move discussion on and, in the end, to bring it to a close. The two Eds left the room at one point to take a call from Gordon, who wanted them to put out statements supportive of the talks, which Paddy Ashdown told him in a call were needed by the Lib Dems to demonstrate that the Labour leadership candidates were behind a coalition.

Primed by Gordon beforehand, both Eds began by saying they were put out by the overnight briefing and messages that they weren't fully behind the talks. On the contrary, they were thoroughly supportive; they wanted to see agreement and a coalition, and they were keen to make progress. Danny responded with good grace. This might have been the prompt for a constructive meeting, but it was not to be.

Danny tabled a single-page note entitled 'Some Areas of Concern', which, because it was far shorter than the thirteen-page updated policy note we tabled, became the agenda for the meeting.

Danny's note listed eighteen policies or areas which, he said, were 'sticking points to any agreement'. It started with the economy, stating: 'swifter action to tackle the deficit, willingness to hold an Emergency Budget'. Peter opened on this by saying that, as agreed, Vince and Alistair were meeting at 11 a.m. to discuss an economic package before it came back to the negotiators. Danny responded that there had clearly been a misunderstanding; the 11 a.m. meeting had been cancelled by them 'because only this group is negotiating on our behalf'. (Vince and Alistair did meet in the afternoon, but it was by then too late to affect anything.) Having got off to this negative start, we agreed to discuss the economy at the end, which ensured a negative end to the discussions too.

However, moving on to constitutional reform proved equally unrewarding. Andrew Stunell began with a speech about how much the Tories were giving them, but how little we were offering; how the Tories weren't 'trapped' by the mentality of government into defending their previous commitments 'as you are' and how we needed to 'get real' and 'raise your offer considerably' if we wanted to 'stay in the game'. He said the Tories were now even offering more on electoral reform. When I asked for specifics, Danny and Chris Huhne rowed back on the statement that the Tories were offering more on electoral reform. This led to the first of Peter's text exchanges with Danny, sitting opposite him across the large round conference table, asking whether Andrew might be a bit more civil so we could make progress. Danny nodded, and showed the message to Andrew sitting next to him.

Following on from the previous night's discussion on the Alternative Vote, I said we could not agree to bring AV legislation into force before a positive referendum vote, as the Lib Dems had suggested, but we were open to there being an additional question on the ballot paper on full proportional representation if they wished. We would make the referendum and AV legislation an issue of confidence, so it would definitely be carried.

We started going down other items on the Lib Dem list of eighteen. Next was Lords reform: 'What will be the electoral system? Will this be put in a separate bill to the AV referendum bill to prevent it being tied up in the Lords?' Yes, I said; and we were prepared to offer proportional representation for a fully elected Lords using a regional list system, which satisfied the Lib Dems immediately. Yet again star billing was given to 'the Wright proposals' for reform of the timetabling of government bills in the Commons, which led Harriet to make all the same points as the previous evening.

Another of the eighteen headings was 'Contact Point', a data system for tracking children's progress and any social services interventions, which the Lib Dems said they wanted to abolish but which only David Laws, Ed Balls and I knew anything about. This provoked Ed into a great defence of Contact Point and a re-run of arguments for and against it, which he and David had had previously in their education briefs. I have little doubt we could have agreed to abolish Contact Point as part of a coalition deal had we considered it with Gordon beforehand or afterwards as one of the eighteen decisive obstacles to a coalition agreement. But we didn't and it clearly wasn't.

Continuing down the list of eighteen, I said we would not proceed on the Heathrow third runway without Lib Dem agreement. There was then a long discussion between Chris and Ed Miliband on nuclear power and targets for renewable energy, and between Ed Balls and David Laws on the pupil premium and how the £2.5 billion cost would be paid for and whether the Tories had agreed to protect the schools baseline, as we would do, both of which turned into debating sessions without firm conclusions.

This took us into the economic discussion, which was a straight re-run of the previous evening's debate on the case for and against further and faster deficit reduction, and how the £10,000 tax threshold would be funded. Ed Balls, David Laws and Chris Huhne went into full debating mode on this, and on public-sector pensions, and little progress was made. By now it was clear that radically accelerated deficit reduction would be a sticking point between us, and this issue would have to be resolved by the leaders together with Alistair and Vince.

As this went on, Peter passed me a note: 'I do not believe they are serious. Laws and Stunell clearly already gone to Tories. How do we sum up? I suggest you list all areas/ items we have overlap/agreement on so as to max. our offer and then we adjourn.' Which we did at 12.30, with Peter and Danny agreeing they would discuss next steps after the next Nick–Gordon meeting, set for 1 p.m.

Before we broke, there was a telling final exchange. I suggested our respective policy staff put together a single text of a coalition deal for the next meeting, highlighting points agreed and outstanding. Danny said this would not be necessary. I suspected he didn't intend or expect there to be another meeting.

•••

There was little time to debrief, but none of us pretended it had gone well. On the other hand, the only obvious policy show-stopper was 'further and faster deficit reduction', if this meant big extra cuts; and we continued to think that Clegg and Cable would hardly want to make this the centrepiece of a progressive coalition.

Harriet left for the party headquarters at Victoria Street for a conference call of officers of the National Executive Committee. This backed talks with the Lib Dems and agreed to plans for a 'Clause 5' meeting on the following Sunday to ratify any coalition agreement.

If the party leadership and executive were holding firm behind the talks, the wider party was visibly splintering.

David Triesman, the party's former General Secretary, texted me at lunchtime to say that Labour would be 'murdered' if it went into a coalition. 'The looming next election will send us into the wilderness. I can see no upside to this.' Andy Burnham became the first senior minister to express overt opposition when on *The World At One* he said that David Blunkett had spoken earlier with 'real authority', adding: 'I think we have got to respect the results of the general election and we can't get away from the fact that Labour didn't win.'

But Nick Clegg had still finally to make up his mind, Tory or Labour. As Peter and I briefed Gordon in his room in the Commons before his 1 p.m. meeting with Nick Clegg, he remained confident he could rally Labour behind a coalition if this was the course Nick Clegg himself finally favoured. This was the meeting to find out.

•••

It was to be their final meeting. For an hour, alone, in armchairs in the corner of the Prime Minister's large L-shaped room in the Commons, they went to-and-fro on the coalition options, with Nick Clegg insisting that a Labour coalition remained a real possibility for him while Gordon hammered away at the problems Nick would have, not least on Europe, if he went in with the Tories rather than Labour.

According to Gordon's account to me later, Nick began by saying that the negotiations had gone 'badly' and he had been told there was a 'lack of commitment' on the part of some of Labour's team. Gordon said if this was the case, why didn't the two of them bring together their negotiating teams, also including Vince and Alistair, to go through all the outstanding issues? Nick didn't want this. 'There isn't really a policy issue between us,' he said. He repeated this line on the phone later: there wasn't a policy obstacle to a Labour coalition, it was more about legitimacy and 'workability'. 'Freshness' was a major theme. 'It's not just you. Lots of your people look exhausted after thirteen years in the trenches.'

Gordon moved onto the principles behind any coalition. A Lab–Lib coalition would be pro-Europe, pro-Keynesian, pro-industrial policy, pro-fairness. Where would Nick be with the Tories? On Europe, where would he be in the first crisis where possible treaty changes or joint economic action was the issue? This Europe point unsettled Nick. 'I am worried about the Conservatives on Europe,' he said, a point he repeated in phone calls with Gordon later in the afternoon.

On the shape of a coalition, Gordon said he wanted it to be an enduring progressive alliance. He saw it as leading naturally to an electoral pact at the next election, with the two parties standing down in favour of each other in some seats. 'This is an historic opportunity for progressive politics which may not come back for fifty years,' he said.

Nick said he would be 'working out what I should do' during the course of the afternoon before a 5 p.m. meeting with his MPs and it would be a 'really, really difficult decision'.

Nick was worried about the Murdoch media: how they had gone on the attack simply because he was talking to

Labour and what they would be like if the two of them went into coalition. (Tuesday morning's *Sun*, under the headline 'SQUAT A MESS' had Nick Clegg's 'shenanigans' provoking 'uproar as the nation began to lose patience with the third party's dithering backbenchers in the face of an economic crisis'. *The Times* deployed the rapier: 'It is quite possible that we will look back on yesterday as the moment the Liberal Democrats demonstrated they are totally unsuited to the serious business of government ... Having said repeatedly that the party with the most seats and the most votes has the right to govern, Mr Clegg's volte-face is bordering on the dishonourable.') There wasn't much comfort GB could offer on that score, except to note that the Murdoch papers would ultimately turn against the Lib Dems either way because they would want the Tories to win the next election outright.

With Nick again saying he needed the afternoon to weigh up his options very carefully, they parted, agreeing to speak on the phone before the 5 p.m. meeting of the Lib Dem MPs.

•••

As Gordon returned to No. 10 at 2 p.m., the Lib Dem negotiators were entering the Cabinet Office through 70 Whitehall to meet the Conservatives for the fourth time.

At first we thought that the Lib Dems were continuing to keep both options open. Nick Clegg had said as much to Gordon only moments earlier, and Paddy was fairly positive in an early-afternoon call with Gordon. We considered what to do in a third round of talks, and prepared a revised policy note to table, starting with the substantial areas of common ground. But as the Lib Dem–Tory meeting lengthened and the pro-Tory briefing from Lib Dems strengthened, the inevitability of a Tory-led government seemed increasingly irresistible. By late afternoon, both Sky and BBC News 24 were broadcasting from opposite walls of the No. 10 war room that a Tory–Lib Dem deal was imminent and GB's resignation could come as early as the evening.

Inside the war room, the moment of truth came shortly after 3.30 p.m. when Alistair Darling came into the war room to report on his delayed meeting with Vince Cable, which had just finished. 'It was all thoroughly cordial,' said Alistair. 'We had barely a disagreement on Budget issues, including phasing in their £10,000 tax allowance gradually – he said it would be mad to do otherwise. But he said it was all beside the point because they were set to go in with the Tories and only the details remained to be sorted. Nick simply didn't think it could be made to work with us, and it was going so well with Cameron. It's all over.'

I texted Paddy shortly afterwards asking if this was true. No response. But Ming Campbell, the most pro-Labour and pro-Gordon of the senior Lib Dems, erased any lingering doubts when Gordon spoke to him on the phone at about 4 p.m. Ming said that the 'outbursts' of Reid, Blunkett et al. had made a strong impression on Lib Dem MPs. How was a coalition without a secure majority going to survive if Labour was so split to start with? Gordon gave a set of reasons why this wasn't the case, and why Reid and Blunkett were unrepresentative. 'But there it is I'm afraid, Gordon,' said Ming, clearly dejected. 'I wish it were otherwise.' Gordon called Vince Cable, who said much the same.

'OK,' said Gordon, putting the phone down. 'I'll do the call with Clegg at five. Get everything ready for the Palace immediately afterwards.'

Amidst all this, Gordon's hairdresser arrived for his weekly trim. 'It's turning into rather a big day,' he said to her as she dodged around the chairs and people in the inner office.

•••

Sarah Brown had been planning the leaving of No. 10 for weeks with calm efficiency. She even hired the same removal firm used by the Blairs three years previously. They had done such a good job of loading every last personal item into the removal truck, boxed and covered to avoid embarrassing photos.

At about 3 p.m. Sarah took Sue Nye, Justin Forsyth and Jeremy Heywood into the Chancellor's study in No. 11 to choreograph the departure. They were anxious that the departure should be in daylight. The last words to the staff would be in the war room, not the grand upstairs pillared room as for TB's resignation. The staff would line the route from the war room to the No. 10 front door. Sarah decided to take the children with them to the Palace and include them in the photos at the front door. The Browns had completely shielded six-year-old John and three-year-old Fraser from the media, but they wanted them to have pictures with their parents as they left Downing Street for the last time.

The last scenes were to be made memorable by Martin Argles, the *Guardian* photographer who followed Gordon for much of the campaign, who appeared in the war room in mid-afternoon and caught the final scenes. This had not been planned. Sue instinctively felt it would be a fitting finale and just phoned him to come. It produced the remarkable portrait of Gordon's final moments in the war room, hugging Fraser, who with John had been pulled up onto a desk to get a view of their father making his emotional farewell speech, surrounded by assorted ministers and the No. 10 team. 'That's Nick and David,' Gordon joked, to a peal of laughter, as two phones rang in unison at one point. Virtually everyone was in tears or on the verge. The Sky News screen was visible on one wall, running the strapline: '19.12: Breaking News: Gordon Brown To Resign As Prime Minister Tonight'.

'The picture that says it all,' wrote Ian Jack when it was reproduced. 'It is a record of how Labour's thirteen years in power ended that includes three great architects of its early success: Mandelson, Campbell and a TV screen.'

Kirsty McNeill and Alastair Campbell set to work on the resignation speech and a speech to party workers at Victoria Street for after the audience with the Queen. Drafts came in and out of the inner office. The resignation speech was finalised with minutes to go before its delivery from the steps of No. 10, Kirsty in tears at the screen and Alastair dictating behind her shoulder. Two desks along, a Foreign

Affairs Private Secretary was making discreet arrangements for David Cameron's congratulatory calls from President Obama and other world leaders after he arrived in No. 10. Another civil servant had a 'transition plan' document up on the screen. It was 7 p.m. The transition of power was palpable.

•••

However, until a few minutes before 7 p.m., uncertainty reigned. It looked as if the death throes of the government could extend overnight or even longer. Until the last moment, extinction itself wasn't absolutely certain.

First, there was the audience with the Queen to be arranged. A meeting of the Privy Council, in the presence of the Queen, had been fixed for 5 p.m. With unchanging routine this had to go ahead, and there was to-ing and fro-ing about when thereafter a resignation audience could take place. So bizarrely, at 4.45, with the government on the verge of resignation, Peter Mandelson – for one of his many offices was Lord President of the Council, requiring attendance at Privy Council meetings – left for the Palace, where the Queen in Council declared a Royal Proclamation for a new 50p coin to commemorate the London 2012 Olympics, and promulgated an Order for the discontinuance of burials in Holy Trinity Old Churchyard, Buildwas, Shropshire. Such was the final official business of thirteen years of Labour government.

Nick Clegg had still not told Gordon that he intended

to go in with the Conservatives. We were by now taking this decision for granted, but it proved elusive to obtain and it was never actually communicated. On the contrary, in three increasingly anguished phone calls, Nick insisted that he was still undecided between Tory and Labour and urged Gordon not to resign. But it was increasingly clear to Gordon that he was being spun along and that enough was enough.

Nick had been due to call before a 5 p.m. meeting of his MPs. As negotiations with the Tories in the Cabinet Office extended, the call did not come, so at 5.30 Sue phoned Nick's office, who put him through.

Gordon said he was going to have to resign at once if there was now no reasonable prospect of a non-Tory government being formed. 'Nick, I can't cling onto power, you must appreciate that.'

'I'm really sorry, but I still haven't taken a decision,' was Nick's opener. 'Genuinely, I mean this. I'm sitting here with Vince and the party meeting now isn't until 8.30. The trouble is, every hour someone else on your side comes out of the woodpile to oppose a coalition, and I'm not sure that your party can deliver.'

Gordon said that the party would come behind him. 'The issue, Nick, is – is there going to be a progressive realignment? This is the historic decision.'

Nick reverted to the negotiations not having gone well. 'I was slightly bewildered by the report back from this morning.' Gordon reiterated that he was sure he could deliver the party behind a coalition. 'Look, I gave up my leadership to make this possible.' He again suggested that they both call their two negotiating teams together to crunch through the issues, but Nick again didn't want this and repeated that it 'isn't really about policy'.

Gordon reverted to Europe. What would happen if there was a deepening European crisis and the Tories refused to engage? 'Our relationship with Europe will be damaged and if you are in with them, there'll be another election by the end of the year.'

'Then we're stuffed,' said Nick.

Gordon came back to Labour and why he was sure he could deliver.

'The trouble is that your party is knackered after thirteen years in power,' Nick responded. 'Some people are up for a realignment but some people aren't.'

They went round the houses again on the issues at stake, touching again on the Murdoch press. Nick realised that 'the stakes could not be higher', that he felt 'great respect' for Gordon. 'If only we'd had these conversations two years ago,' he said.

Gordon returned to the point: he had to have a decision now on whether Nick was serious about a Lab–Lib coalition or he would have to resign at once. The position had become unsustainable.

Nick said he needed to meet colleagues and his parliamentary party again before he could make his decision.

'I can't wait that long, Nick. I can't wait the whole evening,' Gordon said, urgent, insistent. 'The country expects a decision.'

'Just two or three hours then,' said Nick, almost pleading. 'I can't be bounced into this.'

Alastair, the two Eds and I, sitting a few feet from Gordon in the inner office, started vigorously shaking our heads at the mention of 'the whole evening'.

'That won't work, Nick…' Gordon started to say as Peter and David Muir rushed in from the war room, where they had been listening in to the call. David stood directly in front of Gordon, raised a single finger and mouthed 'one hour, one hour, that's it', followed by a cutting sign with his hands.

'One hour, Nick, that's as long as I can leave it. It really is.'

'OK, one hour then.'

•••

As Gordon put the phone down, Peter said: 'He's made up his mind. It couldn't be clearer.'

'I said I'll give him another hour,' said Gordon. 'Look, he said he genuinely hadn't made up his mind. I tell you, the moment Cameron is through that front door, he goes up 10 per cent in the polls. I've got to keep at it until it's hopeless. Tony didn't get the peace process done by giving up every time there was a roadblock.'

'It's certainly worth an hour,' Alastair agreed. But we all thought that Clegg was trying to keep Gordon in play simply to get better terms from the Tories, and that this had probably been the case for some time, perhaps all the time.

Kirsty came in with the next draft of the resignation

speech. Gordon went out to the war room to work at it himself on the PC for a few minutes, coming back with Martin Argles, who took photos of the Brown team in different combinations while people cracked jokes to relieve the tension and pass the time.

'Well, at least you won't have to make the same old jokes at the start of every speech,' said Ed Balls. 'Who's heard them all?'

Ed led the way round the room with people retelling GB speech jokes, Gordon contributing the punch lines.

There was the one about the Chancellor and the three envelopes left by his predecessor for opening in times of trouble. The first saying, blame your predecessor. The second, blame the statistics. The third, write three letters to your successor.

And the one about General Montgomery. Asked who were the three greatest generals in history, Monty replied, 'Well, the other two were Napoleon and Alexander the Great.'

GB sat down to write the customary welcome note to the new Prime Minister. 'How do I start?' he asked out loud. 'How about, "Dear David and Nick…"'

He called Tony Blair. All warmth and passion spent on both sides. 'I am sorry we fell out; I know it could have been better…'

Aides wandered around No. 10 for memory's sake. TB's old office next to the Cabinet Room was set up with new desk and chairs for David Cameron. Trophy photos were taken sitting at Cameron's desk.

•••

6.30 came and went. Still no Clegg call.

Would it make the slightest difference? Almost certainly not, but what was he playing at? Alastair was giving the BBC's Nick Robinson regular text updates with 'colour' to keep the TV commentary going. 'Gordon Brown and his colleagues are putting a brave face on things in No. 10; they have been telling jokes…' Robinson said, standing outside the front door.

•••

At 6.45, Sue put another call through to Tim Snowball in Nick Clegg's office.

'I'm sorry, he's in a meeting and I can't get him out,' said Tim.

'It's really got to be now, Tim. It absolutely has to be,' said Sue.

Thirty seconds' silence then Nick on the line.

'Gordon, I'll tell you what's happening,' Nick began. 'Following our conversation this afternoon' – i.e. their 1 p.m. meeting in the Commons – 'I'm basically finding out how far I can push the Conservatives on Europe. I genuinely take to heart what you said about that. We need some sanity on Europe. We can't seek to renegotiate. I'm trying my best…'

Gordon interrupted. 'I need to resign immediately, Nick. I can't leave this hanging. I can't be hanging on to power while we can't get an answer.'

'But Gordon, this isn't over yet…'

'Nick, you are continuing formal negotiations with the Conservatives and you have rejected a deal with us.'

'No, Gordon. Today is Tuesday. We have only just started the talks. We have not rejected you. We are trying to play our role, to find a stable coalition.'

'I have to do the right thing by both the Queen and the country,' Gordon continued, coming back again to the need for a decision after five days of uncertainty. 'You are still talking to the Conservatives so I'm assuming you will form a coalition with them.'

Nick again said he hadn't made up his mind. 'As you know, the working group weren't able to answer some of our questions…'

'Nick, it's past that. I have to resign as people don't understand my clinging on to power.'

'Why? In other democracies trying to do this it takes weeks. It's quite right for us to do it methodically.' His big concern remained Europe, he added.

'You and I have agreed the issue between us is not one of substance, it's one of legitimacy and workability,' he continued. 'You and I are not the parties that got most votes…'

'Nick, you're a good man. But I have to respect the British people. They don't want me hanging on. I wish you well in the future. I think your decisions are important. I prefer the progressive way forward…'

Nick interrupted, reverting yet again to the negotiations not having gone well, particularly on the economy.

More shaking of heads in the inner office. David Muir texted Jonny Oates: 'He is not bluffing.'

Gordon: 'Nick, I've got no choice. I have thought through the implications, I cannot go on for another day. You are negotiating with another party…'

Nick, dramatically: 'Just five minutes, five minutes. There are two more people I have to speak to. Then let's speak again. Please.'

Pause. Gordon: 'Five minutes. Then I have to go to the Palace.'

A collective groan in the inner office as the line went dead.

•••

The No. 10 staff were now crowding into the war room, along with Sir Gus O'Donnell and senior Cabinet Office officials.

Five or so minutes later, Nick Clegg again. 'Gordon, I cannot give you assurances. That would be acting dishonourably. But please, please don't resign…'

'I can't delay. I've got to resign now, Nick. I need to go to the Palace.'

'You are holding me hostage. You don't need to act unilaterally. We have only spent five days holding these important negotiations. I can't do anything about that…'

'No, Nick. I've got to go the Palace. I've got to resign. I haven't got any choice now.'

'It doesn't need to be like this…'

'It does, Nick, I've got to resign. It's got to be now. I wish you all the best for the future. You're a good man, Nick. I've got to go now.'

EPILOGUE

At 7.19 p.m. Gordon Brown left No. 10 for Buckingham Palace to resign.

At 8.45 p.m. David Cameron arrived at No. 10 from the Palace. 'I aim to form a proper and full coalition between the Conservatives and the Liberal Democrats,' he announced immediately.

At half-past midnight Nick Clegg announced that Lib Dem MPs had voted to support his proposal for a coalition with the Tories. 'I would like to thank David Cameron for the very positive, constructive and workmanlike way in which we have been able to reach a basic agreement over the last few days,' he said.

THE COALITION
AND BEYOND

CAMERON-CLEGG: THREE YEARS ON

5 *Days in May* was written in the heat of battle. Re-reading it after nearly three years, it reminds me of a general's despatch after one of Britain's all too common defeats in the Napoleonic wars, dictated while the smoke was still swirling and the dead and maimed being taken off the field. It is vivid, partisan, and angry about the perfidy of Albion's supposed allies, in this case Nick Clegg and the Lib Dems.

The sense of intense, seismic drama I felt during the five days has not dimmed.

Even as I get older, I don't remotely agree with Arthur Balfour's dictum that in politics 'nothing matters very much and few things matter at all'. On the contrary, politics matters very much. It matters to citizens whose lives are to a considerable extent at the mercy of decisions and policies of government and other public authorities. And it matters, fundamentally, to the character and morality of society, which is shaped by the behaviour of its political leaders as surely as it is by its economic, scientific and cultural leaders.

Few short periods in politics have mattered more in

Britain than those five days in May, and few have pulsated more at the time. Secret meetings day and night; ceaseless plotting and planning; helicopters whirring overhead while packs of television cameras swarmed back and forth across Westminster and Whitehall. It was *West Wing*, *Borgen*, the lot: a raw battle for power to decide not only who would govern but which political leaders would survive and which would be brutally discarded, and which big policies would win or lose, including fundamental changes to the rules of the game – major constitutional reforms tossed across negotiating tables – which would shape the political battle thereafter.

How does it look in hindsight, three years on? In these two supplementary chapters, I look back – in wider perspective – on the five days that produced the Cameron–Clegg coalition.

In retrospect I downplayed Labour fatalism during and after the 2010 election, but I do not alter my view that the decisive factor in the formation of the Cameron coalition was Nick Clegg's decision to back the Tories rather than Labour immediately after the election. I also reaffirm my view that a Lab–Lib coalition would have been viable, although only on the basis that the Lib Dems categorically refused to install a Tory-led government (which was of course not the case).

I conclude that Disraeli was right and England still does not love coalitions, although it can live with them if need be. I suggest how coalition might be more successful in future, learning from the performance of Nick Clegg and the Lib Dems in the present coalition. But I hope coalition is not necessary after the next election. I believe Britain would do best with a One Nation Labour majority government. So I set out the challenge for Labour to recreate a successful One Nation coalition within itself, rather than relying on a coalition from without.

Labour fatalism

My account of the five days in May is reticent about the state of the Labour Party in 2010.

This reticence is exemplified by the one instance of deliberate toning-down in the text. This is Peter Mandelson's remark to me at Labour's deserted headquarters on the morning of election day, when I was trying to persuade him to take seriously the prospect of a hung parliament and negotiations with the Lib Dems which might start within only a few hours. I relate Peter as saying: 'Look Andrew, it's simply not going to happen. If the country wakes up on Saturday morning and Labour is still there, there will be a wave of national revulsion.' In fact what he said to me was: 'Look Andrew, it's simply not going to happen. If Gordon Brown is still Prime Minister on Saturday morning, there will be a wave of national revulsion.'

Anti-Gordon remarks, often bitter, were two-a-penny during the five days, including from his closest colleagues. A significant portion of the Labour Party seemed to be treating the general election as a way to resolve the leadership question. This was exacerbated by the strong sense, even after the closer-than-expected result, that Gordon lost the election and had been personally rejected. But it was also pent-up frustration, in some cases animosity, brewing for years.

Post-election memoirs and interviews by Gordon's former
Cabinet colleagues don't leave much unsaid. As one who
had been among Tony Blair's closest aides, while working
cordially with Gordon after 2007, I found it bewildering.

However, re-reading *5 Days*, it is what I don't say at all
– rather than what I tone down – that is more significant.
In particular, I don't relate that in 2009/10 a fair proportion of the Labour Cabinet were resigned to losing the
election. And when the election wasn't won by the Tories, they
were equally resigned to handing power to David Cameron
on a plate.

Gordon never gave up. On the Friday after the election,
and over the weekend, he was determined to remain Prime
Minister if at all possible. He didn't only want to form a
Lab–Lib coalition: he wanted to lead it. In his discussions
with Nick Clegg on the Sunday and Monday, where his
personal position was a key issue, Gordon traded ever-
diminishing terms of office in return for a Lab–Lib coalition.
By Monday, after an embarrassingly personal discussion
with Clegg on the Sunday evening, it was down to a transition period of just a few months. But Gordon's starting
position was a far longer transition of eighteen months or so.
His view was that he needed to stay until key economic and
constitutional measures had been implemented. In particular, he argued to Clegg that a change to the voting system, to
introduce the Alternative Vote, simply wouldn't get through
the Labour Party and a referendum without him.

Had Gordon resigned the Labour leadership immediately
on the Friday morning, and announced that he intended to

take no role in a Lab–Lib government apart from negotiating its birth, this might have made it harder for the Lib
Dems to go into coalition with the Tories. It would have
blunted David Cameron's 'big, open and comprehensive'
offer to the Lib Dems on the Friday afternoon, which
instead became the key power play immediately after the
election. It would also have removed one of the ostensible
reasons Nick Clegg gave for favouring the Tories – namely,
Gordon's continuation.

However, Gordon made no such move, and no one in
Labour's high command suggested it. They just expected
that coalition talks would run into the sand, and then
Gordon would go. The will to power was not there.

Herein lay Labour's deeper problem in May 2010. The
party was exhausted, demoralised, almost leaderless, with
many ministers and MPs anxious to escape into opposition
and stay there for a good while recuperating. Thirteen years
in government had drained them dry.

Two subsequent events on Wednesday 13 May – the sixth
day after the election and the day after David Cameron took
office – exemplified this Labour fatalism. First was a meeting
of the shadow Cabinet at lunchtime. Gordon had by now
resigned the Labour leadership and the main issue was the
timing of a leadership election. Most of those who spoke
favoured an early leadership election so that a new leader
could be in place by the end of the summer, able to lead
strongly at the party conference and the return of Parliament
in the autumn. However, this was promptly overruled by the
party's National Executive Committee in favour of a longer

leadership election running until the party conference at the end of September. A long dose of introspection was the order of the day.

An hour after the shadow Cabinet there was a packed meeting of the Parliamentary Labour Party in the Gladstone Room of the House of Commons. Almost all the speakers roundly condemned the decision even to negotiate with the Lib Dems. One speech sticks in my mind, although I cannot recall the speaker. 'We lost the election. By getting out now, we can regroup and we will be back soon. This lot won't last five years, no chance. The last thing we wanted was a coalition with the Lib Dems,' he said, to loud applause.

At the time, I too thought that the Cameron–Clegg coalition would not last five years. I was sitting at the back of the PLP meeting finishing – on my Blackberry – an article for the following day's *Guardian* arguing that the Cameron–Clegg coalition was like the infamous Fox–North coalition of the 1780s: a coalition of convenience, uniting opposites, precarious from the start and liable to disintegrate at any moment. 'If it lasts five years, water will start to flow uphill,' I wrote, perhaps unwisely.

However, I thought that the result of an early collapse of Cameron–Clegg would be a snap election which the incumbent Tories would win on a 'stable government' and 'give us a chance' ticket. By contrast, if there were an early second election with Labour as the incumbent, fought under a fresh Labour leader in place of Gordon Brown, I thought this would be far more likely to lead to a Labour majority, for the same reason.

The key point here is that I believed at the time – and I still believe – that a Lab–Lib coalition was viable in May 2010, and that Labour could well have won the subsequent election. This is so strongly against the conventional wisdom which most of the political players sought to establish in May 2010 and subsequently that I need to explain it more fully.

The road not taken

Tellingly, the two people who grasped the reality of power best during those five days in May 2010 were David Cameron and Gordon Brown. It is why Cameron made his big coalition play for the Lib Dems on the day after the election – a 'thunderbolt', as I describe it in *5 Days in May* – and why Gordon responded in kind.

David Cameron understood the imperative to get into No. 10 at almost any price – in fact, the price turned out to be modest – and this meant doing all he could to stop the Lib Dems acquiescing or collaborating in the continuation of a Labour government. Cameron knew that once he had the keys to No. 10, his room for manoeuvre, and his power of initiative, would be massively enhanced. Indeed, his own survival as party leader probably depended upon it. The election result was bad for the Tories and for Cameron personally, but it appeared far less bad once he was waving outside No. 10 and dispensing loaves and fishes. As Gordon never stopped saying during the five days, once Cameron was in No. 10, and together with the Lib Dems branding 'the last, failed Labour government' as the cause of all ills, it would be 'worth 10 points in the polls and make it almost impossible to get him out in one term'.

Labour should have fought with every sinew in 2010 to retain power. To give up power voluntarily, because you are tired of government and it is all too difficult, is a betrayal of the people you serve. In politics, exhaustion and attrition need to be overcome, not indulged.

It was claimed at the time, and has since become a piece of conventional wisdom, that 'the numbers didn't add up' for a Lab–Lib coalition. In truth, the numbers were there, provided the Lib Dems went Left rather than Right and Labour was disciplined. The key numbers were these: Labour plus Lib Dem 315; Tory 307; other parties – almost all of them far more anti-Tory than anti-Labour – 28. On the basis of statements made by the minor parties during the five days, not one of which said they would vote to put the Conservatives in office or vote to cause an early second election, a Labour–Lib Dem coalition would have had a majority of about thirty in the key initial 'confidence' votes tabled by the Conservatives on the Queen's Speech and a Budget. The closest approach to such a high-stakes vote in the present parliament, when the Lib Dems voted with Labour in January 2013 to delay the redrawing of parlia-mentary boundaries beyond 2015, saw the Conservatives lose by 334 to 292, a majority of 42.

A Lab–Lib majority would have been vulnerable, after these initial confidence votes, if the minor parties were to have united against the coalition on an issue of confidence. An early second election might have been forced. But this would almost certainly not have happened until at least a year after May 2010. The Northern Irish DUP had no love for the Tories (who had stood against them in 2010 in league with the UUP), while the Scots and Welsh nationalists had an overwhelmingly strong interest in avoiding a general election before – or at the same time as – the elections to the Scottish Parliament and Welsh Assembly in May 2011. It would have been political death for either of the nationalist parties to have been instrumental in creating a Tory government in London, and they were both united in wanting to divorce the Scottish and Welsh devolved elections from any general election, which would be fought as an essentially Labour/Tory contest.

From Labour's perspective, a Lab–Lib coalition, with the possibility of an early second election, was a risk well worth taking. Not only would it have kept the party in power, but Labour had a good chance of winning a second election, even if it came in 2011 or 2012.

Success in an early second election would largely have turned on Labour's capacity to project new and better leadership after Gordon Brown. During the five days in May, the historian in me was mindful that changes of Prime Minister in 1963, 1976, 1990 and 2007 all created game-changing opportunities for unpopular governing parties. One such change (John Major succeeding Margaret Thatcher in 1990, when the Tories had been in office for more than eleven years) led to the governing party's re-election. Another (Gordon's own succession of Tony Blair in 2007 after ten years in office) would probably have done so had Gordon called an early election. The third (Alec Douglas-Home succeeding Harold Macmillan in 1963 after twelve years in office) brought the Tories very close to re-election in 1964. And the fourth precedent (James Callaghan succeeding Harold Wilson in 1976) might easily have helped Labour to re-election, rather than the election of Margaret Thatcher, had Callaghan gone to the polls before the fateful 'winter of discontent' in 1978–9.

It was therefore not pre-ordained that Britain should have taken the Tory road in 2010. Only in the light of what actually happened does that now seem inevitable.

However, back to May 2010, although Labour fatalism helped put the Tories in office, the critical determinant was Nick Clegg's instinct to go Right rather than Left.

The Lib Dems veer Right

Given the way events unfolded on the day immediately after the election on 6 May 2010, the only credible outcome to the five days of inter-party discussions was a Tory government in some form. This is because Nick Clegg signalled precisely such an outcome, and his desire for it, in two ways. First, he strongly legitimised the Tories over Labour by peddling a constitutional doctrine – of no historical or international validity – that he felt bound to seek agreement if possible with the party that had won the largest number of seats. Second, he opened negotiations with the Conservatives alone on the day after the election, which reinforced his preference for the Tories over Labour. These moves not only gave legitimacy and momentum to the Conservatives; they also immediately and fatally weakened Labour support for a Lab–Lib coalition.

There could have been a radically different dynamic, leading to a Lab–Lib coalition, had Clegg instead said, the day after the election, that the key issue in the election had been economic policy; that on this issue the Conservatives had been decisively rejected (by 15 million votes to 10 million); and that he would not therefore be prepared to install or sustain a Conservative government. Supporting the second largest party in Parliament in this way would have been entirely within accepted constitutional practice, in Britain and other parliamentary democracies. In this event, a continuing Labour government with Lib Dem support – probably a coalition – would have been almost certain, partly as a matter of compatibility but also because no other government would have been possible. In these circumstances the only alternative would have been an immediate second election, which virtually no one – even in Labour's most defeatist ranks – wanted or thought desirable. And as I noted above, the parliamentary arithmetic made a Lab–Lib partnership viable.

Clegg turned Right, not Left, and a Tory-led coalition was the result. However, it is as clear to me in retrospect as it was at the time that a Lab–Lib government would have been viable if it had been presented from the outset as the only combination that respected the wish of the great majority of voters, and a majority of MPs, to pursue Alistair Darling's economic policy rather George Osborne's. Since the Lib Dems had fought the election squarely on the Darling plan

– and in opposition to the Osborne plan – this would have been a legitimate, defensible and credible course of action.

Why did Clegg turn Right? Because, on the big economic questions, he is on the Right, not the Left; and so too is David Laws, his chief strategist.

Political parties are driven by ideas, leaders and antipathies in about equal measure. Under Nick Clegg and David Laws, all three led the Lib Dem leadership to the Right in the run-up to the 2010 election, although this was not reflected in the party's published policies.

David Laws's book on the formation of the coalition – *22 Days in May*, published in December 2010 – is retrospectively clear and unapologetic about this rightward shift, and it is crucial to understanding why the May 2010 election yielded a Tory-led government. (Laws's '22 days' start with the five post-election days and continue for the seventeen days he was Chief Secretary to the Treasury.)

David Laws became an MP in 2001, following a career in banking and finance. *The Orange Book*, which he edited with a fellow financier, Paul Marshall, in 2004, was a clarion call for a return to classical small-state liberalism. In his essay in the book, entitled 'Reclaiming Liberalism', Laws defined this reclamation as an unambiguously neo-liberal project. 'How did it come about,' he asked rhetorically, 'that over the decades up to the 1980s the Liberal belief in economic liberalism was progressively eroded by forms of soggy socialism and corporatism, which have too often been falsely perceived as a necessary corollary of social liberalism?'

In *22 Days in May*, Laws identifies *The Orange Book* as

helping 'to shift the centre of gravity in the party ... from big-government solutions and from tax-and-spend'. It was but one part of a wider intellectual shift. Tellingly, John Stuart Mill, the apostle of classical nineteenth-century liberalism, was the subject of an adoring biography published in 2008 by Richard Reeves, who became principal adviser to Clegg as Deputy Prime Minister in May 2010.

In the early months of the coalition, I was struck by how much support these views had among younger Lib Dems, who came of political age under Blair and Brown. At a discussion in autumn 2010 of 'Lib Dem ideas' at the Institute for Government, younger speakers were full of 'the failure of the social-democratic experiment', arguing – in classic Tory/Liberal mode – that a small state would enhance both prosperity and fairness.

The key point is that Clegg and Laws did not lead their party into coalition with the Conservatives *despite* Osborne austerity but *because* of it.

In *22 Days in May*, Laws was explicit about his neo-liberalism and how this led him naturally towards the Conservatives. 'I believed that a Lib Dem–Conservative coalition could be capable of delivering the "tough but tender" economics which I had long believed in, and which would be essential in dealing with the Budget deficit,' he wrote. He noted with particular approval that in the coalition agreement, 'where the parties had [previously] differed, we had generally decided on one policy or the other'. On the economy, this was George Osborne's policy for eliminating the structural deficit within a parliament, a policy

immediately taken forward by Laws as Chief Secretary to the
Treasury, 'the job I wanted more than any other', he added.

An Osborne–Laws mutual admiration society was crucial
to the formation of the coalition. In his book, Laws recalled
Osborne's pre-election attempt to persuade him to change
parties, with a promise from David Cameron of a Cabinet
seat if he did so. Laws declined, but he did not disguise
his pleasure at working with Osborne. The Lib Dem–Tory
relationship was 'astonishingly positive and constructive', he
wrote (that was autumn 2010), and he lavished praise on the
'bright, sharp and amusing' Osborne and his 'extraordinary
strategic and tactical understanding of British politics'.

Antipathy to Labour also drove the Lib Dems rightwards.
This wasn't just about Gordon Brown and electoral tactics in
Lib–Lab marginal seats. In two sentences in *22 Days in May*,
Laws condemned New Labour and virtually all its works:

> Many Lib Dems were [by 2010] as disenchanted with
> Labour as they had earlier been with the Conservatives. The
> war in Iraq, the undermining of civil liberties, the endless
> centralising and micro-managing, the failure to embrace
> radical constitutional reform ... and the lack of progress on
> social mobility and improving public services...

I find this passage extraordinary. In May 2010, Iraq was long
past, and against these airy negatives could be set swathes of
policy strongly supported by the Lib Dems at the time: the
renovation of the NHS, the minimum wage, the Climate
Change Act, the Human Rights Act, Sure Start, Building

Schools for the Future, tens of thousands more teachers, doctors and nurses, devolution, equal rights, international development and so on. But objective judgement isn't the issue. What matters is that by May 2010 Clegg and Laws were prepared to assert the 'failure of the social-democratic experiment' as an article of faith. Tellingly, they called themselves 'liberals', not 'social democrats', in contrast to the previous generation of Lib Dem and SDP leaders.

Laws highlighted Nick Clegg's election as Lib Dem leader in 2007 as being 'of particular importance' in paving the way to a coalition with the Tories. 'Nick was the first leader for decades who felt genuinely equidistant in his attitude to the other two parties,' he noted. Clegg's Continental liberal pedigree – ambiguous in its public positioning before he had to make straight Left/Right choices in 2010 and subsequently – led him decisively rightwards with Laws on the crucial economic agenda, where Continental liberals of the Dutch and German FDP variety also veer Right. This set him apart from the previous generation of progressive-Left SDP and Lib Dem leaders, from Roy Jenkins and David Steel to Paddy Ashdown, Charles Kennedy and Ming Campbell.

Social democrats – including ex-Liberal Democrats like me – failed to appreciate this at the time. We knew that Nick Clegg had a Dutch mother and had been a Eurocrat. But until Chris Bowers's biography of Clegg, published in 2011, most of us hadn't realised that his political and personal background put him so clearly on the political Right. All his formative political associations were on the Right, notably his years working as adviser to the EU's trade commissioner,

Leon Brittan, a stalwart of the Thatcher Cabinet in the 1980s. And his wife was not simply Spanish, but the daughter of a Spanish Conservative parliamentarian.

Until Clegg became an MP in 2005, after five years as an MEP, he 'had very little knowledge of Britain politically', writes Bowers. As an MEP he was 'more ... a Continental liberal than perhaps a mainstream British liberal', Chris Davies, a Lib Dem MEP colleague, told Bowers. Andrew Duff, another fellow Lib Dem MEP, put it thus: 'If the Conservative Party had been how it used to be under Edward Heath, Nick would be a Tory, albeit a natural liberal, pro-European Tory like Chris Patten and Ken Clarke.'

Leon Brittan told Bowers that Clegg decided to go for a Lib Dem nomination to the European Parliament because he 'didn't like Labour at all and didn't like the Conservatives enough [as] he was very unhappy with the Conservatives' European policy'. Ed Vaizey, another Tory friend, put it still more explicitly: Clegg was 'essentially Tory but divided by one issue, in his case, Europe'.

However, Bowers stresses that being pro-European did not make Clegg less of an economic liberal. On the contrary, he quotes the journalist John Palmer, who knew Clegg well in Brussels, and who links Clegg's Europeanism to his neo-liberalism. 'His work with Leon [Brittan] in and around the single market and competition policy probably had quite a strong influence on him. He was quite markedly to the Right of some of his colleagues,' said Palmer.

Bowers paints a picture of Clegg's background which, Europe apart, fits Cameron like a glove – in wealth, education, outlook, style, the lot. The English side of Clegg's family could hardly be more Tory Establishment. The son of a wealthy Buckinghamshire banker, educated at prep school and Westminster like his grandfather (his father was at Bryanston), Clegg emerges as a privileged Home Counties, public-school boy, in largely the same mould as David Cameron and George Osborne. Laws's social and educational background is similar.

Without this personal and political context, it is hard to fathom what happened during the five days, and why Clegg and Laws plumped for a Tory rather than a Labour coalition.

Economic policy was the essential Labour/Tory dividing line in the post-election negotiations. And the key point to emerge from Laws's *22 Days in May* – as from my account in this book – is that Laws and his fellow Lib Dem negotiators did not seek to negotiate with the Conservatives on the central issue of economic policy, namely the pace of deficit reduction. They simply accepted Osborne's plan for eliminating the structural deficit within a single parliament, in preference to Alistair Darling's less austere policy of halving the annual deficit within a parliament.

Why did Clegg and Laws open discussions with Labour at all during the five days? Partly for tactical reasons. For their own party, the irreducible minimum policy requirement of a coalition was to secure a referendum on electoral reform, the holy grail of Liberal politics since Lloyd George. In the first day of negotiations with the Tories, this was the main sticking point. It was essential to bring Labour into play to put pressure on the Tories to give ground on electoral reform.

Once this was achieved – on the evening of Monday 10 May (Day Four after the election), when Cameron conceded a referendum on the Alternative Vote electoral system – a Lab–Lib coalition became a redundant option to Clegg and Laws. Having accepted Tory economic policy, there was no reason whatever to contemplate the far tougher political task, given the parliamentary arithmetic and the necessity of dealing with Gordon Brown, of seeking to form a Lab–Lib coalition, only to achieve a less drastic deficit-reduction policy which they did not want anyway.

Clegg, Laws and their team also thought it critical to be able to claim – particularly to Left-leaning Lib Dems – that Labour could not have made a coalition deal stick in any event. It was important for them that talks with Labour should start but appear to fail. My account is starkly at variance with Laws's on this point and I stand by mine. By the end of Day Four the Lab–Lib talks had not failed; rather, they were unilaterally abandoned by the Lib Dems. Hence the aspersions about Labour's negotiating style – made at the time and repeated by Laws in *22 Days in May* – to provide an excuse.

Laws also claimed that Labour was not serious about negotiating economic policy because Alistair Darling was not part of the negotiating team. But neither was Vince Cable, the Lib Dem Treasury spokesman, part of the Lib Dem team. It was for this reason that, as related in my account, Gordon Brown suggested on Sunday (Day Three after the election) that Cable and Darling meet to discuss deficit reduction. Such a meeting was arranged between Cable and Darling for the following morning, but when Clegg and Laws discovered this, they had it delayed and it only took place on the afternoon of the Tuesday, shortly before Clegg and Cameron agreed the terms of their coalition, by which time it was clearly superfluous and treated as such by the participants. In his book, Laws described the intended Cable–Darling meeting as 'another Gordon Brown wheeze'. Yet Cable agreed to it readily enough, and had he and Darling been tasked with drawing up a credible economic plan, I doubt they would have had difficulty agreeing one.

As an appendix to *22 Days in May*, Laws published a selection of documents from the negotiations. There is a significant omission. While the paper tabled by Labour for the Lib–Lab talks is there, the paper tabled by the Lib Dems is absent.

I publish the Lib Dem paper in the appendix (page 181). Re-reading it, it is not hard to see why Laws did not wish it to be published. It refers to 'a commitment not to raise the cap on tuition fees', 'immediate legislation to introduce the Alternative Vote' without a referendum, 'a commitment to no public subsidy for nuclear power stations', 'a cut in the number of government ministers', a four- (not five-) year fixed-term parliament, and other items of subsequent embarrassment. However, in retrospect it is more significant that even in this paper there is a commitment to 'the eradication of the structural deficit within a responsible timescale', which, Laws explained in our meetings, would need to be a timescale significantly shorter than envisaged either by Labour or the Lib Dems in their election manifestos. The 'deteriorating situation in Greece', a possible run on the pound and UK debt were the reasons given. This became the chief policy bone of contention in our one session of serious discussions with the Lib Dems on the Monday (Day Four) after the election.

At the time I didn't think the Lib Dems were serious about backing the Osborne plan. I thought they were looking to split the difference somewhere between Osborne and Darling. This was wrong. Laws and Clegg were clearly intent on backing the Osborne plan, and they have stuck to it in the three years since.

It is equally telling that in *22 Days in May*, published during the Tory–Lib Dem honeymoon in autumn 2010, Laws was open to the possibility that the coalition might continue beyond the current parliament. He did not even rule out a Lib–Con electoral pact for the 2015 election. While he described this as 'highly unlikely', he stressed that 'it will take many years to deliver on the programme and the aspirations which the coalition has set out so far'. 'This is a coalition formed in the tough times of fiscal retrenchment, one which has the potential to be a partnership for the good times, too,' he wrote.

For Nick Clegg and David Laws, coalition with David Cameron and George Osborne was a marriage of neo-liberal minds. This, fundamentally, is why it was possible to form the Tory–Lib Dem coalition in the first place, and why it has survived for the subsequent three years.

FROM COALITION TO ONE NATION

The lessons I take from the three years of coalition government since 2010 are fourfold.

- First, it is possible to make coalitions work in modern Britain, and for them to be as stable as single-party governments.
- Second, in a future hung parliament, coalition is therefore likely to be a serious option, provided the Lib Dems have enough seats to give one or both of the larger parties a majority. All three parties need to prepare properly for this eventuality – only the Conservatives did so in 2010 – while of course campaigning for an outright majority.
- Third, coalition is not a superior form of government to single-party majority government.

This is a sobering lesson for pragmatic social democrats like me who in the past thought that coalition, as a form of government promoting consensus and unity, might be stronger and more effective than single-party government. Instead, since 2010 we have had an almost undiluted Conservative government – entirely undiluted in its core economic policy – plus a few, largely random, Lib Dem vetoes and delays in lesser areas. Far from being more than the sum of its parts, the Cameron–Clegg coalition is not even the sum of its parts. Tellingly, public support for coalition as a form of government has plummeted since autumn 2010.

- Fourth, Nick Clegg went into government but not into coalition, which is why Lib Dem influence is so weak.

Nick Clegg has played a poor hand within the coalition. He made two strategic mistakes at the outset from which he has not recovered: he failed to take significant ministerial posts for himself and his lieutenants; and he made constitutional reform – a change to the electoral system and an elected House of Lords – the essential Lib Dem policy contribution to the coalition. Since these constitutional reforms, having little popular support and being largely about the political self-interest of the Lib Dems, proved fairly easy for the Conservatives to subvert, it is the Tory social and economic programme, overseen almost exclusively by Tory ministers, which dominates the coalition and will be its legacy. As a result of these two structural faults, Clegg went into government but not into coalition.

Coalition has become deeply unpopular with most Lib Dems and Conservatives, which is the most graphic evidence of its weakness.

Back in the Downing Street rose garden in May 2010, coalition was touted as an enduring Tory–Lib Dem partnership.

There was even speculation, by leading figures on both sides, of a joint policy programme for 2015 and a possible electoral pact. No one talks like that now. Lib Dems blame the Conservatives for destroying their constitutional reforms, chafing at Osborne austerity yet without any alternative to offer. Tories blame the Lib Dems for diluting or delaying parts of their programme, and are publicly and privately contemptuous of a weak coalition partner whose only value to them is votes in the Commons.

Far from contemplating a renewed coalition, the Conservatives are staking out a policy programme with plenty of 'clear blue water' between themselves and the Lib Dems, particularly on Europe, welfare and economic policy. There is now no possibility whatever of joint policy positions, let alone an electoral pact, in 2015.

So, England still does not love coalitions. As a necessity they can work, and they need to be prepared for. But for the two major parties, they are the product of electoral and policy failure. For the Left, this makes Labour's One Nation strategy all the more important. Labour must seek to win on its own, and to do so as an effective progressive coalition within itself.

Coalition government and progressive politics

I used to think coalition government was preferable to single-party government. But I have changed my mind in light of experience over the last thirty years, culminating in the Cameron–Clegg coalition.

For a pragmatic social democrat, the case for coalition

between parties of the centre-Left and the centre is super-
ficially attractive. The argument goes thus. Believers in a
social market economy and an open, liberal society are
spread across all three major parties. On key issues – such
as Europe, civil rights, balancing economic dynamism and
social protection, and public service reform – they may
have more in common with progressives in other parties
than with the extremes of their own party. Coalitions might
therefore promote consensus behind mainstream social
market policies, and make governments stronger and better.

This view was popular in the 1970s and 1980s, when I
was coming of political age, because of the extremist drift
of both the Labour and the Conservative parties and the
foundation of the Social Democratic Party (SDP), intended
by its founder Roy Jenkins to strengthen what he called the
'radical centre'.

So central was coalition government to Jenkins's thinking that the very existence of the SDP – which I joined as
an eighteen-year-old founder member in 1981 – depended
upon an electoral pact with the Liberal Party. The SDP
stood down in favour of the Liberals in about half of all
constituencies in the 1983 general election. Jenkins set up
the SDP, rather than simply joining the Liberal Party and
encouraging fellow social democrats to do so too, because
he thought this was more likely to strengthen the centre-Left
and showcase coalition politics.

'Some form of coalition is essential for democratic leadership,' Jenkins argued in his Dimbleby Lecture of autumn
1979. 'Sometimes the coalitions are overt, sometimes they

are covert. I do not think the distinction greatly matters. The test is whether those within the coalition are closer to each other, and to the mood of the nation they seek to govern, than they are to those outside their ranks.'

Reflecting the depth of divisions within Labour and the Conservatives at the time, Jenkins argued that 'big tent' parties of Left and Right 'make the moderates too much the prisoner of the extremists'. He added, with some bitterness, of his experience in dealing with Tony Benn and the Labour Left in the 1970s: 'I would much rather that it [coalition government] meant overt and compatible coalition than that it locked incompatible people, and still more important, incompatible philosophies, into a loveless, constantly bickering and debilitating marriage, even if consecrated in a common tabernacle.' He ended with Yeats's lament: 'The best lack all conviction, while the worst / Are full of passionate intensity.'

This was a fair argument from the vantage point of 1981. And had the SDP–Liberal Alliance held the balance in the 1983 parliament, able to change the electoral system to proportional representation, making inter-party coalitions unavoidable, then it might have been vindicated. But something very different happened.

Instead, the SDP, with its Liberal allies, failed to make an electoral breakthrough in 1983 and fell back further in 1987. Far from being a strength, the existence of two separate parties, with separate leaders and programmes, rapidly became a hindrance and after 1987 the two parties voted to merge and become a single conventional party. This was itself a retreat from coalition politics. Furthermore, it only happened after severe bloodletting within the SDP, which demonstrated, first, that bitter infighting with an ideological edge is not the preserve of large broad-church parties (small parties, including centrist parties, are just as prone to it); and second, that centre 'liberal' parties generally contain as broad an ideological spectrum of activists as parties of the Left and Right. In the case of the Lib Dems, the spectrum of views even among the party's MPs range from the Left of the Labour Party to the Right of the Conservative Party, with plenty in each camp, as witnessed by the debate on *The Orange Book* since 2004. And being a small party preoccupied by survival, they prioritise constitutional reforms in their political self-interest rather than broad social and economic policy, about which they are anyway sharply divided.

All of these characteristics are exhibited in sharp relief by the Lib Dem participation in the Cameron–Clegg coalition. They largely explain why the Lib Dems have been so weak a force either for moderation or for reform within government.

Furthermore, to return to the 1980s, the extremist drift of the Labour Party turned out to be a passing phase. From the mid-1980s, under Neil Kinnock, John Smith and Tony Blair, Labour moved to the centre-Left and developed a credible social democratic reformist mission. However, it did so by leadership from within, not by coalition from without. By the advent of the Blair government, the extremists had become the prisoner of the moderates, not the other way around. So much so that Roy Jenkins himself became a close confidant and adviser to Tony Blair while the superfluous Lib Dems remained on the opposition benches after New Labour's landslide in 1997. To paraphrase Yeats, it was the best, not the worst, who acquired all conviction and passionate intensity. (Ironically, Jenkins came to fear that Tony Blair possessed rather too much of both by the time of the Iraq invasion.)

The Conservatives also moved to the centre after the defenestration of Margaret Thatcher in 1990, although less decisively, and John Major proved unable to contain Tory infighting on Europe beyond a truce sufficient to win the 1992 election. This shift, too, had nothing to do with external coalitions. Indeed, fast forward to the coalition in 2013 and the striking point is the inability of the Lib Dems to moderate the Conservatives – their coalition partner – on any major aspect of policy, not least economic policy or European policy. On economic policy, Nick Clegg does not even wish to be a moderating force. On Europe – the cause of serious last-minute angst on Clegg's part during the five days in May – he tried but failed to stop Cameron committing to an in/out referendum. Tory policy could hardly be more Eurosceptic had the party won a landslide in 2010.

There is another point of context. The 'Labour Right' and the 'Tory Left' ran out of ideas, leaders and governing competence in the 1970s. This is why Margaret Thatcher and the Right, and Tony Benn and the Left, took over or came close to taking over their respective parties. Tellingly, Roy Jenkins's lecture cited earlier was entitled 'Home thoughts from abroad'. He delivered it while President of the European Commission, having decamped to Brussels after losing the battle for the Labour leadership in 1976, four years after he voluntarily resigned the deputy leadership of the Labour Party. As for Roy Jenkins the brilliant liberal moderniser – as Home Secretary in the mid-1960s – it took place while he was securely in the Labour mainstream, and his very success at the Home Office and afterwards the Treasury made him for a while a serious contender to succeed Harold Wilson. Had Jenkins become Labour leader, I suspect he would have been less keen on founding another party and promoting coalition.

In reality, the best way to advance mainstream progressive politics is to organise, lead and win from inside the major parties. It is a chimera to regard coalition as a means of securing 'external' victory after 'internal' defeat. Coalition may be a necessity where there is no Commons majority for a single party; but it is no more than that.

The Lib Dems are in government, not coalition

The strengths and weaknesses of governments, and their seeds of ultimate demise, can usually be traced to their foun-dations. This is certainly true of the Conservative–Lib Dem coalition.

From the outset, there were two clear strengths. First, the two leaders got on. Cameron and Clegg cultivated good relations in opposition before 2010. This was crucial to the formation of the coalition, as it has been to the weathering of vicissitudes since. The aides and lieutenants of the two leaders have also had fairly good relations, largely in consequence.

Secondly, the two leaders and their key lieutenants agreed on economic policy and have stood behind it confidently, without which the government would have foundered in short order. (The economic policy itself is in my view flawed, but that is another matter.) Tellingly, the one department where the two parties work closely and harmoniously together is the Treasury, where first David Laws and then Danny Alexander as Chief Secretary have worked hand-in-glove as deputy to George Osborne as Chancellor, in both cases as true believers in the Osborne strategy. So much so that Laws spent his seventeen days in the Treasury overseeing emergency cuts while one of Alexander's first acts in the weeks immediately afterwards was to cancel a high-profile government loan to the Sheffield Forgemasters, one of the largest employers in Nick Clegg's own constituency.

By contrast, in other departments either only one minister counts – almost invariably a Conservative, even where policy is controversial (notably Michael Gove at Education and William Hague at the Foreign Office; the same was true of Andrew Lansley at Health until 2012) – or, in the few cases where there is a Lib Dem Secretary of State, they are deliberately 'man-marked' by a hostile Tory and there is endemic tension between ministers of the two coalition parties (notably between Ed Davey and his Tory deputy, John Hayes, at Energy and Climate Change (DECC), and between Vince Cable and his Tory business and employment affairs deputy Michael Fallon at Business, Innovation and Skills (BIS)).

This highlights the first big weakness of the coalition as a coalition: that hardly any Lib Dem ministers count.

This weakness starts at the top. Nick Clegg's decision in May 2010 to become Deputy Prime Minister without leading a major department, basing himself in the Cabinet Office with constitutional reform as his only portfolio, has given him little leverage within the government. The idea was that, shorn of departmental responsibilities and bias, he could better oversee all departments, like the Prime Minister. But the Prime Minister wields the resources and authority of No. 10, the Cabinet Secretary and his position as chair of the Cabinet, ministerial head of the civil service and leader of the major party. The Prime Minister also treats bilaterally with overseas leaders, represents Britain alone in the European Council and controls most of the levers of patronage and appointment. The Deputy Prime Minister has little or none of this power.

Clegg's mistake was to believe that simply by virtue of being leader of the second coalition party, his power would be institutionalised across government. At the point at which the government was formed, his power was indeed potent, in respect both of personnel (ministerial appointments) and policy (the coalition agreement), because the government could not have been formed without his assent to each. But since that moment, the Cabinet Office has been a weak base for the Deputy Prime Minister. The Cabinet Office is not a powerful department in its own right; nor is it integrated with No. 10 to give the Deputy Prime Minister a meaningful share of prime ministerial power. Perhaps Nick Clegg thought that proximity to No. 10, and his title of DPM and his status as a party leader, would lead to the office of Prime

Minister being divided or shared, but this has not happened. Clegg does not even attend David Cameron's daily planning meetings at 8.30 a.m. and 4 p.m., where the PM, George Osborne, Cabinet Secretary Jeremy Heywood and key No. 10 aides transact the government's key tactical and strategic business day by day. Indeed, no Lib Dem is present at these meetings.

The one attempt at institutionalising Lib Dem influence in No. 10 was the decision in 2010 to make the No. 10 Policy Unit non-partisan, staffed largely by civil servants and reporting both to the Prime Minister and the Deputy Prime Minister. But for this very reason it has been marginalised and ineffectual.

In my post-election discussions with Gordon Brown in May 2010 about the shape of a possible coalition with the Lib Dems, I took it for granted that Nick Clegg would install himself in a major department and stamp his policy and Lib Dem branding upon it. Either the Foreign Office or the Home Office seemed obvious, given Lib Dem priorities. This would have followed Continental coalition practice of the leader of the second coalition party taking a key portfolio, typically the Foreign Ministry in Germany. I was strongly in favour of this. From my experience of Whitehall, where Deputy Prime Ministers based in the Cabinet Office without portfolio (like John Prescott between 2001 and 2002) have been powerless, it was clear to me that a strong departmental base, far from distracting the DPM from wider issues, was essential to providing the leverage necessary to impact upon them. Clegg badly lacks this.

Furthermore, the personal portfolio Nick Clegg took with him to the Cabinet Office – constitutional reform – simply reinforced his unsuccessful strategy of putting political reform at the heart of Lib Dem coalition policy.

Clegg's weakness has not been redressed by ministerial strength elsewhere. In my discussions with Gordon about a possible coalition, I suggested that the Lib Dems should take Cabinet posts in each of three key 'sectors' of government – namely, international policy (Foreign, Defence and International Development); at least one of the public service or welfare departments (Home Office, Health, Education, Transport, Work and Pensions, Communities and Local Government, and Culture, Media and Sport); and a 'green' department (Energy and Climate Change or Environment, Food and Rural Affairs), as well as the No. 2 jobs in the Treasury and in other major departments where the Lib Dems were not in the lead. I envisaged the Lib Dems taking four head of department Cabinet posts, with Clegg combining one of them with the Deputy Prime Ministership as just described, plus another lesser Cabinet post or two to give a fair relative balance within a Cabinet of about twenty-five.

This was not so much to secure good posts for the Lib Dems but because I believed a coalition would only be strong and unified if the Lib Dems were thoroughly bound into its ministerial leadership across the Whitehall waterfront. Labour had a keen interest in not short-changing them.

Clegg secured almost none of these major posts in his coalition negotiations with Cameron. It is not even clear that he asked for them, although if he did ask and was refused then he badly underplayed his hand. (This will be a significant point of interest in the memoirs to come.) Of the twelve head of department posts just mentioned, the Lib Dems secured only one – Energy and Climate Change (DECC), which was among the least significant and, for the Lib Dems, the most problematic, given its responsibility for nuclear energy. They secured no Cabinet post whatever in two of the three key government sectors of international policy and public services/welfare, where there are ten departments. Instead, Vince Cable – Lib Dem Deputy Leader at the formation of the coalition, in a wary relationship with Clegg – took the Business, Innovation and Skills department, presumably with a view to being able to influence economic policy, where he is significantly to the Left of Cameron/Osborne/Clegg. However, BIS in practice offers little scope for cutting across the Treasury, as has proved the case since 2010.

BIS and DECC were the only head of department posts secured by the Lib Dems. Their three other Cabinet posts (Chief Secretary to the Treasury, Scottish Secretary and Clegg himself at the Cabinet Office) are either subordinate or non-departmental. (Technically the Scottish Office is a department, but its main job is to shadow the Scottish government, where the power lies.)

It is hard to conceive that the Lib Dems could have negotiated a worse allocation of ministerial posts.

This absence of ministerial clout has rendered the Lib Dems largely unconnected and irrelevant to most of

Whitehall. Government is made up of decisions and policies agreed day by day, week by week, by secretaries of state in charge of departments, sometimes involving discussion and agreement with the Prime Minister and the Chancellor. Virtually all of the players in each of these 'power triangles' are Tories.

Nick Clegg thought he could turn the triangles into squares by supervising all key government decisions from his eyrie in the Cabinet Office, supplemented by bilateral discussions with the Prime Minister as well as through the work of the so-called 'quad' (an informal grouping of Cameron, Osborne, Clegg and Alexander which discusses coalition business, particularly economic policy) and a rejuvenated Cabinet committee system, including a formal 'coalition committee' to resolve high-level differences.

None of this, however, has remotely substituted for the absence of Lib Dem leadership in key Whitehall departments. The best that the Lib Dems have been able to secure in most policy areas is an occasional veto or delaying power on Conservative policy. The Deputy Prime Minister's ability to question decisions or proposed policies – usually on the verge of them being announced – is a long-stop power, and the same is true of Cabinet committees. Tellingly, the coalition committee has barely met since 2010. Furthermore, while Cabinet committee discussion is a good thing (there was far too little collective discussion among ministers in the Blair/Brown governments), this has not served to strengthen the Lib Dems to any notable degree. The story of Andrew Lansley's health reforms, Michael Gove's education reforms,

Iain Duncan Smith's welfare reforms and Cameron/Hague's European policy largely testifies to Lib Dem weakness. As for BIS, three years into the government there is still no 'signature' Vince Cable policy or reform distinct from George Osborne's Treasury. Indeed, the only major reform for which Cable and his department are responsible is the trebling of tuition fees, contrary to the Lib Dem manifesto pledge to scrap them entirely.

In short, in 2010 the Lib Dems went into *government* but not into *coalition*. They handed virtually all the posts that mattered to the Conservatives, and they also – partly in consequence – handed almost all the policy of the government to the Conservatives too.

Having made this initial mistake, Nick Clegg stuck to it in the 2012 reshuffle when he chose to stay in the Cabinet Office rather than taking a major department. Bizarrely, he even kept constitutional reform as his personal portfolio, even after the collapse of electoral reform and House of Lords reform. And he secured no change whatever in the other Lib Dem Cabinet portfolios. He did not even insert a junior minister into the Department for Culture, Media and Sport (DCMS), despite the raging Leveson controversy on press regulation. (Again, it will be interesting to learn from the memoirs whether Clegg asked for different posts and was refused. He was in a much weaker position than in 2010, given ministerial sitting tenants and his generally weaker political position.)

Having secured a precariously narrow foothold in the machinery of government, the only other way Clegg and the Lib Dems could exert influence within the executive was through the formal coalition agreement. However, here again the position of the Lib Dems was very weak because the only significant policy concessions they sought and gained from the Conservatives in the May 2010 coalition agreement concerned constitutional reforms which rapidly crumbled to dust.

To appreciate the scale of this misjudgement, consider the first major speech Nick Clegg made as Deputy Prime Minister, a week after the coalition took office. The subject was constitutional reform. The coalition was going to enact 'the biggest shake-up of our democracy since the Great Reform Act of 1832'. Clegg could hardly have set his sights higher: 'Incremental change will not do: it is time for a whole-sale, big-bang approach to political reform, that's what this government will deliver … a programme so important to me personally that I will take full responsibility for seeing it through,' he declared. It was to be 'our very own Great Reform Act', including 'an elected second chamber where members are elected by a proportional representation' ('the time for talk is over'), a wholesale reform of party funding, and a referendum on electoral reform. 'David Cameron and I are very relaxed about the fact we may be arguing different cases in that refer-endum,' he added, confident that he would win.

Three years later? 'The British public, when they were asked for a change in the electoral system, they did not seem that interested,' Clegg told a Commons committee ruefully in February 2013. As for a new 'constitutional blueprint', that was 'like waiting for Godot – it just won't materialise'.

For the Lib Dems, the chronic weakness of the initial coalition agreement was compounded by the absence of any machinery or timetable to refresh the coalition's programme in mid-term. The Lib Dems needed such machinery because of their junior status within the government. Only by securing at the outset of the coalition – in the founding coalition agreement itself – that this would take place within two years could the Lib Dems have retained significant ongoing policy leverage. However, this did not happen.

Instead the coalition's 'mid-term review' was simply that: a review of progress on the initial coalition agreement, with a list of what was left to do from the 2010 agreement, plus a handful of new departmentally inspired (and therefore mostly Tory) policies. Even this document was repeatedly delayed. It was expected in the summer of 2012, at the end of the first two years of coalition (i.e. half the way through its effective working life, allowing for a lame-duck period in the run-up to a 2015 election). However, it did not finally appear until January 2013, and it was so thin that it made no impact whatsoever.

How to form a coalition
Learning from the Cameron–Clegg experience, it is clear that four things are required for a future coalition to be coalition of substance rather than name:

- The leader of the second party needs to head a major department in his or her own right.
- There needs to be genuinely joint control of economic policy and the Treasury.

- The second party needs to hold at least one Cabinet post in each of the three main sectors of the government (i.e. foreign/defence; public services and welfare; environment/energy).
- There needs to be robust machinery for ongoing policy development and negotiation between the parties.

Above all, to make a genuinely joint programme viable, there needs to be a sufficient identity of interest and policy, rather than a Tory–Lib Dem coalition of opposites held together by mutual fear of the ballot box.

However, this is all second best. First best is for Labour to win outright as a broad-based progressive party, informed by the best thinking in other parties and beyond but not reliant on coalition with other parties to assemble a majority in the Commons.

This requires One Nation Labour.

One Nation Labour

The Conservatives did not win the 2010 election, hence the 'five days in May' and this book.

The Tories fell well short of a House of Commons majority. They secured a smaller proportion of constituencies than any 'winning' party since Ramsay MacDonald's Labour Party in the hung parliament of 1929. Even Harold Wilson did better in the election of February 1974 (the only other 'hung parliament' election since 1929), when Labour's share of the popular vote was lower than for Edward Heath's

Tories but Labour won 47.4 per cent of the seats compared to 47.2 per cent for the Conservatives in 2010.

The Tories feel cheated by the electoral system. Hence their strategy, derailed by their Lib Dem partners after the defeat of House of Lords reform, to redraw parliamentary boundaries in time for a 2015 election. However, the Tory failure to win a Commons majority in 2010 wasn't just bad luck. At 36.1 per cent, the Tory vote in 2010 was the lowest for a 'winning' party since Britain became a recognisable democracy in 1918, with one important exception (Labour in 2005, at 35.2 per cent).

The root of the Tory problem is that they are no longer a national party. For a generation now, they have barely existed in Scotland and in most of the conurbations of the Midlands and the North. In these large swathes of the country, Conservatives don't fluctuate between winning and losing, they fluctuate around zero. In 2010 they won not a single seat in any of the cities of Manchester, Birmingham, Liverpool, Leeds, Sheffield, Bradford, Newcastle, Nottingham, Leicester, Stoke or Derby. In Scotland they won a mere two seats and in Wales only eight.

Even in the cities of southern England, the larger and more socially and racially mixed the city, the worse the Tories do. Labour won decisively more seats than the Conservatives in London (thirty-eight to twenty-eight), sweeping inner London. In Bristol, the biggest city in southern England outside London, the Tories won only one of four seats.

So the Tories have big problems. But Labour's are equally big, because the biggest concentrations of population and dynamic energy in the country are in the south, and beyond London and Bristol, Labour won barely any seats in southern England.

In 2010, out of 218 seats south of Birmingham excluding London, Labour won only ten. In the twenty-five counties of southern England, Labour won no seats at all in nineteen (Buckinghamshire, Cambridgeshire, Cornwall, Dorset, East Sussex, Essex, Gloucestershire, Herefordshire, Hertfordshire, Kent, Norfolk, Northamptonshire, Somerset, Suffolk, Surrey, Warwickshire, West Sussex, Wiltshire and Worcestershire).

This weakness in densely populated southern England also explains why Labour did so poorly in the popular vote, polling only 8.6 million votes to the Conservatives' 10.7 million.

Some have suggested that Labour's real problem in 2010 lay in its 'core' constituency of working-class voters, where it also fell back. Or that Labour's predicament is essentially a 'rising tide' issue because its support is 'naturally' weaker in southern England; as the electoral tide recedes Labour is submerged in the south, but when the tide rises again, it will reclaim the territory.

However, this simply re-poses the challenge for Labour to build substantially more support, without which it will not win seats in southern England. In 2010, Labour's national vote fell to 29 per cent. Tony Blair won in 1997 with 43.2 per cent and with 40.7 per cent in 2001. So Labour lost about a third of its support over the following decade. It is important to note that this was not a post-Blair phenomenon

– Labour's vote fell to 35.2 per cent in 2005 – but rather an 'exhaustion and heartlands' effect: as exhaustion and attrition took hold in government, particularly post-Iraq, Labour was pushed progressively back to its heartlands and now has the challenge – as under Kinnock, Foot and early Blair – to become a national party once again.

Put thus, both major parties have the same problem: neither have strong nationwide support. In one respect the Tory predicament is worse, in that their wipe-out in the North and Scotland now appears permanent, whereas for Labour, the recent Blair elections yielded fairly strong support in votes and seats in southern England. Nonetheless, the Labour wipe-out in southern England outside London was near total in 2010, and it will take a dramatic shift in support and perception to reverse it. The Eastleigh by-election of February 2013, where Labour stuck at 10 per cent while UKIP surged to 28 per cent and second place, highlighted this challenge starkly. The necessity to become a party of southern England becomes still greater when the parliamentary boundaries are finally redrawn for the election after 2015, when the balance of seats shifts decisively south.

Ed Miliband is therefore right to advance 'One Nation Labour'. It not only seizes the 'One Nation' mantle from the Conservatives at the point where their credibility as a One Nation party is shot through. It also concentrates Labour's mind on the imperative to become, as in the early Blair years, a One Nation party in social appeal and geographical reach. This requires Labour's philosophy and programme to be avowedly national, not sectarian.

One Nation Labour is a party of aspiration, enterprise and responsibility as well as social justice. It is proudly liberal as well as Labour. It is the party of modernisation not the status quo; of responsibility – personal responsibility, social responsibility, economic responsibility – as well as equality, rights and freedoms.

One Nation Labour speaks the language of Middle England – middle class and working class – which wants to see more and better jobs, more choice and higher standards in the public services, more and better opportunities for their children to get on, and which also wants greater security, both physical security in neighbourhoods and greater security in facing the challenges of modern life.

One Nation Labour does not mean recycling New Labour policies in an unthinking way. Some, like the quest for greater choice and higher standards in education and health, are still appropriate. Others, particularly Labour's approach to financial regulation, growth, infrastructure, welfare and devolution within England – need to change radically in the light of changed circumstances and challenges.

Labour's 1945 manifesto – written amidst the break-up of Churchill's great wartime coalition – seized the One Nation modernisation theme under the inspired title 'Let us face the Future'. Its final chapter was entitled 'Labour's call to all progressives', and it warned: 'It is very easy to set out a list of aims. What matters is whether it is backed up by a genuine workmanlike plan conceived without regard to sectional vested interests and carried through.'

That is our challenge today. To set out not just a list of

aims – one nation, responsible capitalism, more and better jobs – but a genuine workmanlike plan conceived without regard to sectional interests and carried through.

APPENDIX: LIB DEM DRAFT COALITION AGREEMENT WITH LABOUR

Heads of Agreement
Liberal Democrat–Labour Party discussions
9 May 2010

1. Political reform

The new government will adopt a radical, far-reaching agenda on political and constitutional renewal and reform. The programme for government will include:

1.1 Immediate legislation to:
set the date of the next election for the first Thursday in May 2014, and establish the principle of four-year fixed-term parliaments in future;

1.2 bring forward a post-legislative multi-option referendum on alternate voting systems, to include the option of the Single Transferable Vote, no later than May 2011.

1.3 A party funding bill to introduce caps on donations and spending limits as proposed by the Hayden Phillips Committee, as part of wider party-funding reform.

1.4 Full implementation of the proposals of the Wright Commission on reform of the House of Commons.

1.5 The early introduction of a Power of Recall for MPs suspended for serious wrongdoing.

1.6 The implementation of the proposals of the Calman Commission and a referendum on increasing the powers of the Welsh Assembly to be called by 18 June.

1.7 A cut in the number of government ministers and in ministerial pay.

1.8 Regulation of lobbying to include a statutory register.

A Freedom Bill to restore and protect British civil liberties and rights, to include the scrapping of the ID cards scheme and the National Identity Register in its entirety and reform to the National DNA database to match requirements in Scotland.

2.   Economy

The new government will ensure that the health of the public finances is restored as quickly as possible while taking no action to jeopardise the recovery. In light of market concerns further and faster action on the deficit will be taken; this will include some in-year cuts.

2.1 An Emergency Budget will be presented within fifty days of the formation of this government. This Budget will:

- set out overall spending plans to eradicate the structural deficit over an expedited but responsible timescale;
- introduce a new Banking Levy;
- make plans to increase the income tax personal allowance to £10,000 by the end of the parliament, with a significant increase in the personal allowance in 2011–12;
- set out new net lending arrangements with the semi-nationalised banks and make provision for a major loan guarantee scheme;
- set up a commission to investigate the separation of high-risk and low-risk banking;
- make proposals to tackle irresponsible bonuses within the banking sector including a one-year continuation of the bonus tax;
- ensure a portion of identified in-year savings to be spent promoting growth and jobs including the implementation of an eco-cashback scheme and protections for young jobseekers;
- include proposals for the roll-out of green mortgages to improve home insulation;
- include proposals to widen the scale and remit of a national infrastructure bank.

2.2 Following an Emergency Budget a Comprehensive Spending Review will be held throughout the summer, reporting in autumn 2010. This CSR will consult widely throughout the public sector, the private sector and with other interested stakeholders.

2.3 A strategic Defence Review will be held alongside the CSR; this will include a decision on Trident renewal.

While ensuring that the UK maintains an independent deterrent, alternatives to the like-for-like replacement of Trident will be considered. This Defence Review will have strong Treasury input.

3.   Wider social, environmental and public service reform

The new government will adopt a decentralising, reforming agenda in relation to Britain's public services and welfare. It will put the environment and tackling climate change at the heart of its programme. And it will place a high premium on restoring Britain's reputation around the world.

The government programme will include:

3.1   The immediate restoration of the earnings link for pensions, with a triple guarantee, so pensions are uprated from April 2011 in line with earnings, prices or a floor of 2.5 per cent.

3.2   A pupil premium to target additional funding to the million most deprived children. This will be fully funded within three years.

3.3   Substantial increases in freedom for schools and hospitals, devolving accountability through our public services.

3.4   A commitment not to raise the cap on tuition fees.

3.5   A commitment to no public subsidy for nuclear power stations.

3.6 A new target of 40 per cent of energy to be from renew-able sources by 2020.

3.7 A commitment to reduce carbon emissions from the public sector by 10 per cent within twelve months.

3.8 A cross-party commission on finding a sustainable settlement on the funding and provision of social care.

3.9 The ending of plans for a third runway at Heathrow and any further expansion of airports in the South East and continuation of plans for High Speed Rail.

3.10 Extensive roll-out, through local government, of Neighbourhood Justice Panels to widen the use of restorative justice.

3.11 A full public inquiry into allegations of British complicity in torture.

3.12 Localisation of business rates as part of a fundamental review of local government finance reform, which will include review of the House Revenue Account.

An updated version of this document was tabled on 10 May 2010. It included:

- *'Immediate legislation to introduce the Alternative Vote system for all Parliamentary elections including by-elections.'*
- *'Immediate legislation to reform [the House of Lords] to create a fully elected second chamber, elected by propor-tional representation.'*
- *'The main burden of deficit reduction will be borne by reduced spending rather than increases in taxation.'*

THANKS AND
ACKNOWLEDGEMENTS

This book would not exist without the painstaking piec-
ing together of events, meetings and conversations in
interviews with the key participants in the weeks immediately
after the 'five days in May'. I am indebted to Gordon Brown,
Peter Mandelson and key members of Gordon's No. 10
team: Iain Bundred, Justin Forsyth, Joe Irvine, Gavin Kelly,
Kirsty McNeill, David Muir, Sue Nye, Nick Pearce and
Stewart Wood.

Peter Mandelson's notes of meetings between Gordon
Brown and Nick Clegg, and Sue Nye's shorthand notes
of Gordon's phone conversations with Nick Clegg were
especially valuable. Tony Lloyd gave me a good account of
evolving sentiment inside the PLP. A number of Lib Dems
and civil servants also spoke to me, but prefer to remain
anonymous.

This is my second book in two years with the brilliant
team at Biteback. Iain Dale, Sam Carter, Suzanne Sangster,
James Stephens, Namkwan Cho and Katy Scholes did
another great job. So did Adam Tyndall, my researcher.

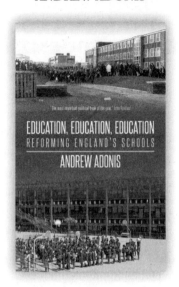